THE One & Only
Cupcakes, Whoopie Pies & Cakepops
Cookbook

THE One & Only Cupcakes, Whoopie Pies & Cakepops Cookbook

METRO BOOKS
New York

METRO BOOKS
New York

An Imprint of Sterling Publishing
387 Park Avenue South
New York, NY 10016

Written by: Wendy Sweetser
Project Editors: Catherine Knight and Martha Burley
Art Director: Susi Martin
Illustrations: Kuo Kang Chen
Publisher: James Tavendale
Photography: All photography by Ian Garlick with the exception of pages 2, 5, 10, 12, 22, 58, 84, 104, 114, 164, 178, 181, 186, 194, 241, 246, 255 (www.shutterstock.com), and page 136 (www.istockphoto.com)

Every effort has been made to credit photographers and copyright-holders. If any have been overlooked, Pulp Media will be pleased to make the necessary corrections in subsequent editions.

ISBN 978-1-4351-4077-6

For information about custom editions, special sales, and premium and corporate purchases, please contact Sterling Special Sales at 800–805–5489 or specialsales@sterlingpublishing.com

Manufactured in China

10 9 8 7 6 5 4 3 2 1

www.sterlingpublishing.com

Contents

Whoopie Pies

Cakepops

Foreword

If you asked me to choose between a cupcake, a whoopie pie, and a cakepop I would probably ask sheepishly if I could have all three, although prudence would probably force me to add "but only one at a time!"

I was therefore delighted to be asked to write this book. If you're like me, and can't choose which sweet treat is your favorite; you'll find the separate chapters will provide you with delicious recipes for all three. Step-by-step instructions are as clear as I could make them to ensure that even the most inexperienced cook will be overjoyed with the results.

The main thing about cupcakes, whoopie pies, and cakepops is that they're not just fun to eat, they're also a delight to make. They appeal to all age groups—they're small enough to fit into a child's palm just as easily as into a grown-up's mouth—and the recipes are endlessly versatile. If you don't like too much sweet frosting on your cupcake, I've included plenty of simple options that taste equally good; many of the whoopie pies have fresh fruit added to fillings; and as for cakepops, nobody could truthfully call them a healthy choice, but they are very small and, hey, everyone deserves a treat sometimes.

So, why not join me in the kitchen? Let's have some fun.

Wendy Sweetser

Cupcakes

Cupcakes

Cupcakes had been around for decades before Sex and the City's Carrie and Miranda agonized over Carrie's love life in New York's Magnolia Bakery and introduced them to millions of new fans. These dainty little cakes have now become so popular that they're seen at almost every celebration; as wedding and birthday cakes in tiers on pretty cupcake stands, to trays of cupcakes baked by home-cooks for school fêtes and neighborhood yard sales.

All the cupcake recipes in this book are easy to follow and require only basic equipment. No special culinary skills are required to make them. The combination of cake mixes and frostings given are only suggestions; if you want to combine the cake mix from one recipe with the frosting from another, simply mix and match flavors as you like.

Basic Equipment

As with any type of baking, you'll need measuring scales, a mixing bowl, measuring pitcher and spoons, a hand-held manual or electric whisk, wooden spoon, grater, cupcake trays, and a cooling rack. Other pieces of equipment—such as a food processor or blender—are useful for saving time and effort but are not essential.

Paper Baking Cups

As any cupcake baker will know, manufacturers don't help the home-cook by supplying standard-sized paper cups. Despite muffin-sized being the most widely available, medium (standard or cupcake) or petit four (mini-cupcake) are also on sale. The size of cups mentioned in these recipes is only intended as a guide to show how many cupcakes were made from the batter. You can substitute different-sized cups, it just means you'll need to adjust the cooking times and will end up with a larger or smaller batch.

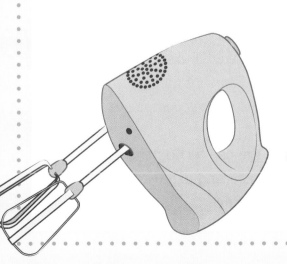

Basic Cupcake Recipe

12 tbsp. (6 oz.) unsalted butter, softened

Scant 1 cup (6 oz.) granulated sugar

3 large eggs, beaten

Scant 1½ cups (6 oz.) self-rising flour

2 tbsp. milk

Makes 12

1 Preheat the oven to 350°F. Line a 12-cup muffin pan with paper baking cups.

2 Beat the butter and sugar together until smooth and creamy. Gradually beat in the eggs, a little a time, adding a spoonful of the flour to prevent the mixture from curdling.

3 Stir in the remaining flour and the milk to make a soft mixture that drops from the spoon when it is lifted.

4 Spoon the mixture into the paper baking cups, filling them about two-thirds full. Bake in the oven for 15–20 minutes or until risen, springy to the touch, and golden brown; or until a toothpick pushed into the center of one of the cupcakes comes out clean.

5 Cool in the pan for 10 minutes before transferring to a wire rack to cool completely.

Basic Buttercream Recipe

This recipe makes a sufficient amount to give 12 cupcakes a medium-sized layering of frosting. If you like a thicker topping you'll need to make more.

10 tbsp. (5 oz.) unsalted butter, softened
2¼ cups (10 oz.) confectioners' sugar
2–3 tbsp. milk

1 Beat the butter until creamy.

2 Gradually sift in the confectioners' sugar, beating well after each addition and adding enough milk to make a soft, spreadable icing.

3 To frost cupcakes, hold a cupcake by its base and top with a spoonful of frosting in the center. Using a small palette knife, spread the frosting over the cake in a circular movement toward the edge of the paper case. Frosting can also be piped onto cupcakes using a piping bag fitted with a star nozzle.

A useful and delicious way to make use of any bananas that have been left to turn brown in the fruit bowl—the riper the fruit, the sweeter and more fragrant the cupcakes will be.

Banana, Blueberry, and White Chocolate Cupcakes

CUPCAKES

9 tbsp. (4½ oz.) unsalted butter, melted and cooled

Scant 1 cup (6 oz.) granulated sugar

½ tsp. almond extract

3 small ripe bananas, peeled and cut into short lengths (about ¾ lb. total unpeeled weight)

4 tbsp. plain yogurt

2 large eggs

2½ cups (11 oz.) all-purpose flour

½ tsp. baking powder

1 tsp. baking soda

3½ oz. dried blueberries

WHITE CHOCOLATE FROSTING

6 oz. white chocolate, chopped

4 tbsp. heavy cream

TO DECORATE

Fresh blueberries

Grated milk chocolate

MAKES 15

TIP If you don't have a food processor, mash the bananas with a fork before stirring or whisking into the melted butter, sugar, almond extract, yogurt and eggs until evenly mixed.

1. Preheat the oven to 350°F. Line a 12-cup muffin pan with paper baking cups.

2. To make the cupcakes, put the melted butter, sugar, almond extract, bananas, yogurt, and eggs in a food processor and blend until smooth. Sift the flour, baking powder, and baking soda into a mixing bowl, add the blended mixture, and stir until combined. Finally, mix in the blueberries.

3. Spoon the mixture into the paper baking cups and bake for 20–25 minutes or until a toothpick pushed into the center of one of the cupcakes comes out clean. Cool in the muffin pan for 10 minutes before transferring to a wire rack to cool completely.

4. To make the frosting, put the chocolate and cream in a heatproof bowl and set it over a pan of simmering water, without letting the bottom of the bowl touch the water. Leave until the chocolate has melted. Stir until smooth. Remove the bowl from the pan and leave in a cool place until the frosting thickens enough to drizzle or spread over the cupcakes.

5. Top the cupcakes with the frosting and decorate with fresh blueberries and a grating of chocolate.

Use dark red or black cherries when they are in season; their fresh, fruity flavor in the cupcakes will contrast well with the sweet icing.

Golden Buttermilk and Cherry Cupcakes

1. Preheat the oven to 350°F. Line two 12-cup muffin pans with 18 paper baking cups.

2. To make the cupcakes, beat the butter and sugar together in a mixing bowl until pale-colored and creamy. Sift the flour, baking powder, and baking soda into a separate bowl.

3. Gradually beat the eggs into the creamed butter and sugar a little at a time, adding a tablespoon of the flour mix to prevent the cake mixture from curdling.

4. When all the eggs have been added, stir in the rest of the flour mix with the buttermilk and cherries until evenly combined.

5. Spoon the mixture into the paper baking cups and bake in the oven for 20–25 minutes or until well risen and a toothpick pressed into the center of one of the cupcakes comes out clean. Cool in the muffin pan for 10 minutes before transferring to a wire rack to cool completely.

6. To make the frosting, sift the confectioners' sugar into a bowl and stir in enough buttermilk to make a smooth mixture that is thick enough to spread over the cupcakes. Before the frosting sets, top each cupcake with half a dried or fresh cherry and multicolored sugar sprinkles.

CUPCAKES
8 tbsp. (4 oz.) unsalted butter, softened
Scant 1 cup (6 oz.) granulated sugar
Scant 2 cups (8 oz.) all-purpose flour
1 tsp. baking powder
1 tsp. baking soda 3 large eggs, beaten
1 cup buttermilk
3 oz. chopped dried sour cherries or pitted fresh cherries

BUTTERMILK FROSTING
1½ cups (6 oz.) confectioners' sugar
3–4 tbsp. buttermilk

TO DECORATE
18 cherry halves, dried or fresh
Multicolored sugar sprinkles

MAKES 18

A delicious variation on the traditional chewy Italian cookies. Crunchy nuts and sticky candied fruits are pressed over the cake mix before baking. Add the white chocolate drizzle for a final flourish.

Florentine Cupcakes

1. Preheat the oven to 350°F. Line a 12-cup muffin pan with paper baking cups.

2. To make the cupcakes, beat the butter and sugar together until soft and creamy. Stir in the honey, then gradually beat in the eggs, adding a tablespoon of the flour to prevent the mixture from curdling. Sift in the rest of the flour, the cinnamon, and the ginger, and stir in with the raisins and golden raisins.

3. Spoon the mixture into the paper baking cups. To make the topping, mix together the almonds, candied cherries, stem ginger, ginger syrup, and pine nuts. Spoon the mixture on top of the cake batter, pressing down lightly.

4. Bake for 20 minutes or until a fine skewer or toothpick pressed into the center of one of the cupcakes between the topping ingredients comes out clean. Cool in the muffin pan for 30 minutes, before transferring to a wire rack to cool completely.

5. Pipe or drizzle the cupcakes with the melted chocolate and let set.

CUPCAKES

12 tbsp. (6 oz.) unsalted butter, softened
Generous ½ cup (4 oz.) granulated sugar
2 tbsp. honey
3 large eggs, beaten
Scant 2 cups (8 oz.) self-rising flour
1 tsp. ground cinnamon
½ tsp. ground ginger
1/3 cup (2 oz.) raisins
1/3 cup (2 oz.) golden raisins

TOPPING

¼ cup (1 oz.) sliced almonds
½ cup (2 oz.) candied cherries, coarsely chopped
1 tbsp. chopped stem ginger in syrup, plus 2 tsp. syrup from the jar
3 tbsp. (1 oz.) pine nuts

TO DECORATE

3 oz. white chocolate, melted

MAKES 12

TIP The candied fruit and nut topping is sticky and will be very hot when it comes out of the oven. It's worth letting the cupcakes cool for longer than usual in the muffin pan before lifting them out, to prevent burning your fingers.

These are the perfect cakes to serve at a summer party or picnic. Fresh raspberries look pretty and add their own special burst of flavor.

Raspberry and Vanilla Cupcakes

1. Preheat the oven to 350°F. Line a 12-cup muffin pan with paper baking cups.

2. To make the cupcakes, beat the butter and sugar together until pale and creamy. Beat in the vanilla and then the eggs, a little at a time, adding a spoonful of the measured flour to prevent the mixture from curdling. Stir in the remaining flour.

3. Gently crush the raspberries with a fork and dust with a little extra flour before stirring into the batter. Let the mixture stand for 10 minutes before dividing between the paper baking cups and baking for 15–20 minutes or until golden brown and springy when pressed. Cool the cupcakes in the muffin pan
for 10 minutes before lifting out and transferring to a wire rack to cool.

4. To decorate, whip the cream with the vanilla until it holds its shape. Pipe or spread the cream over the cupcakes and top with extra raspberries and small fresh mint leaves.

CUPCAKES
8 tbsp. (4 oz.) unsalted butter, softened
Generous ½ cup (4 oz.) granulated sugar
1 tsp. vanilla extract
2 large eggs, beaten
*Scant 1 cup (4 oz.) self-rising flour, plus a
    little extra for dusting*
1 cup (4 oz.) fresh raspberries

TO DECORATE
Scant 2/3 cup (5 fl. oz.) heavy cream
½ tsp. vanilla extract
Extra raspberries
Small mint leaves

MAKES 12

TIP Dusting the crushed raspberries in extra flour and letting the cupcake mixture stand for 10 minutes to thicken a little will help prevent the raspberries from sinking during baking.

You could substitute apricot jelly for the fine-shred marmalade if you're not a fan of the peel. If you're devoted to those tangy "bits," try coarse-cut marmalade, available in specialty baking stores.

Tangy Orange and Almond Cupcakes

CUPCAKES

12 tbsp. (6 oz.) unsalted butter, softened
Scant 1 cup (6 oz.) granulated sugar
2–3 small seedless oranges or
  3 clementines
3 large eggs, beaten
Scant 1 cup (4 oz.) self-rising flour
1 tsp. baking powder
½ cup (2 oz.) ground almonds
4 tbsp. orange marmalade (fine-shred)

TOPPING

4 tbsp. orange marmalade (fine-shred)
3 tbsp. finely chopped pistachios

MAKES 12

1. Preheat the oven to 350°F. Line a 12-cup muffin pan with paper baking cups.

2. To make the cupcakes, beat the butter and sugar together until creamy. Finely grate the zest from one of the oranges or clementines and beat into the creamed mixture. Mix in the eggs, a little at a time, adding a tablespoon of the flour to prevent the mixture from curdling. Sift in the rest of the flour with the baking powder and stir in with the ground almonds.

3. Spoon half the batter into the paper baking cups and top each with 1 teaspoon of marmalade. Cover with the rest of the batter. Peel the oranges or clementines, remove any loose pith, and cut into thin slices. Lay the slices on top of the cupcakes and bake for 20–25 minutes or until a toothpick pushed into the center of one of the cupcakes comes out clean.

4. Cool the cupcakes in the pan for 10 minutes before transferring them to a wire rack to cool completely.

5. To make the topping, warm the marmalade until it melts, then brush it over the tops of the cupcakes. Sprinkle with the pistachios and serve warm or cold.

These are a great way to get kids into the kitchen to prepare for their Halloween party. The cupcake mix is easy enough for little ones to try and they'll love making the marzipan decorations.

Pumpkin and Hazelnut Cupcakes

1. Preheat the oven to 350°F. Line a 12-cup muffin pan with paper baking cups.

2. To make the cupcakes, sift the flour, baking soda, and cinnamon into a mixing bowl and stir in the sugar and hazelnuts. Beat together the melted butter, eggs, orange juice, and orange zest and add to the bowl. Stir well until evenly combined, then stir in the pumpkin purée.

3. Divide the mixture between the paper baking cups and bake for 15–20 minutes or until golden brown and a toothpick pushed into the center of one of the cupcakes comes out clean. Cool in the muffin pan for 10 minutes before transferring to a wire rack to cool completely.

4. To make the chocolate buttercream, beat the butter until soft. Gradually sift in the confectioners' sugar, beating well each time and adding the cocoa powder with the last addition of sugar. Stir in enough milk to make a soft, spreadable icing.

5. Spread the buttercream over the top of the cupcakes. Decorate with small pumpkins shaped from orange gum paste or marzipan with green stalks and black features (or buy Halloween pumpkin candy).

CUPCAKES
Scant 2 cups (8 oz.) self-rising flour
1½ tsp. baking soda
1 tsp. ground cinnamon
1 cup (7 oz.) light brown sugar
1 cup (4 oz.) hazelnuts, chopped
10 tbsp. (5 oz.) unsalted butter, melted and cooled
3 large eggs
1 tbsp. orange juice
Finely grated zest of 1 orange
¾ cup (6 oz.) pumpkin purée, unsweetened (see Tip)

CHOCOLATE BUTTERCREAM ICING
10 tbsp. (5 oz.) unsalted butter
2 cups (9 oz.) confectioners' sugar
1 tbsp. cocoa powder
2–3 tbsp. milk

TO DECORATE
Pumpkins molded from orange, green, and black gum paste or marzipan

MAKES 12

TIP You can buy unsw
purée, or make your ov
a wedge of pumpkin, di
Cut into chunks and ste
or until very tender. Coo
towel, then mash with a

You can make these seductive treats as hot as you like by varying how much chili you use. Remember, the smaller the chili, the hotter it is likely to be.

Dark Chocolate and Chili Truffle Cupcakes

1. Preheat the oven to 350°F. Line a 12-cup muffin pan with paper baking cups.

2. To make the cupcakes, put the chopped chocolate in a heatproof bowl with the milk and set the bowl over a pan of simmering water. Leave until the chocolate has melted, stirring until smooth. Remove the bowl from the heat to cool a little.

3. In a mixing bowl, beat the butter and sugar together until creamy. Beat in the egg yolks one at a time, then stir in the melted, cooled chocolate. Sift in the flour and baking powder and stir in with the chopped chili. In a separate bowl, whisk the egg whites until stiff. Stir 1 tablespoon of egg white into the chocolate mixture to loosen it, then carefully fold in the rest.

4. Spoon the mixture into the paper baking cups and bake for 20 minutes or until firm to the touch. Cool in the muffin pan for 10 minutes before transferring to a wire rack to cool completely.

5. To make the frosting, dissolve the sugar in the evaporated milk in a pan over a low heat. Bring to a boil and simmer for 2 minutes. Remove from the heat and stir in the chopped chocolate until melted. Stir in the butter and vanilla and then beat until the frosting is smooth and shiny. Transfer to a bowl and let cool completely, stirring occasionally.

6. Spread or pipe the frosting over the cupcakes and decorate with gum paste or marzipan chilis and sugar sprinkles.

CUPCAKES

6 oz. dark chocolate, chopped

3 tbsp. milk

10 tbsp. (5 oz.) unsalted butter, softened

¾ cup (5 oz.) light brown sugar

2 large eggs, separated

Scant 1½ cups (6 oz.) all-purpose flour

1½ tsp. baking powder

1 fresh chili, deseeded and very finely chopped

CHOCOLATE FROSTING

6 tbsp. (3 oz.) granulated sugar

1/3 cup (3 fl. oz.) evaporated milk

5 oz. dark chocolate, chopped

3 tbsp. (1½ oz.) unsalted butter, cut into small pieces

1 tsp. vanilla extract

TO DECORATE

Chilis molded from red and green gum paste or marzipan

Red or green sugar sprinkles

MAKES 12

Simple cupcakes lifted to the heavens with a topping of vanilla buttercream studded with bright gum paste stars. If you don't have a star cookie cutter, use a small sharp knife to cut out the gum paste. Don't worry if the edges aren't perfectly even, the cakes will still twinkle on the plate!

Star-Spangled Vanilla Cupcakes

1. Preheat the oven to 350°F. Line a 12-cup muffin pan with 10 paper baking cups.

2. To make the cupcakes, beat the butter and sugar together until pale and creamy. Gradually beat in the eggs, a little at a time, adding a tablespoon of the flour to prevent the mixture from curdling.

3. Stir in the rest of the flour with the vanilla extract until evenly combined. Divide the mixture between the paper baking cups and bake for 15–20 minutes or until the tops of the cupcakes are golden and springy to the touch. Let the cupcakes cool in the pan for 5 minutes before transferring to a wire rack to cool completely.

4. To make the buttercream, beat the butter until soft. Gradually sift in the confectioners' sugar a little at a time, beating well after each addition. Stir in the milk and vanilla. Pipe or spread the buttercream over the tops of the cupcakes.

5. To decorate, roll out colored gum paste thinly on a board lightly dusted with confectioners' sugar. Cut out small stars using a sharp knife or a star cutter. Dust the tops of the cupcakes with red sugar crystals, then gently press the stars into the buttercream.

CUPCAKES

8 tbsp. (4 oz.) unsalted butter, softened
Generous ½ cup (4 oz.) granulated sugar
2 large eggs, beaten
Scant 1 cup (4 oz.) self-rising flour
½ tsp. vanilla extract

VANILLA BUTTERCREAM

8 tbsp. (4 oz.) unsalted butter, softened
1¾ cups (8 oz.) confectioners' sugar
1 tbsp. milk
½ tsp. vanilla extract

TO DECORATE

Small amounts of colored gum paste icing
Confectioners' sugar, for rolling
Red sugar crystals

MAKES 10

TIP Colored sugar crystals are available from cake decorating suppliers, or you can make your own by putting a couple of tablespoons of granulated sugar into a small plastic food bag and adding a little powdered food coloring. Seal the top of the bag and shake well until the sugar is evenly colored.

You could substitute fresh cranberries for dried in these delicately flavored cakes. Simmer fresh cranberries with very little water for a few minutes until they "pop," then drain, pat dry, and dust them with a little of the flour before adding to the mix.

Cranberry, Pecan, and Ginger Cupcakes

CUPCAKES

12 tbsp. (6 oz.) unsalted butter, softened
Scant 1 cup (6 oz.) light brown sugar
3 large eggs, beaten
Scant 2 cups (8 oz.) self-rising flour
1 tsp. ground ginger
6 tbsp. (2 oz.) dried cranberries
½ cup (2 oz.) chopped pecans
2 tbsp. milk

MAPLE SYRUP FROSTING

1½ tbsp. maple syrup
3 tbsp. (1½ oz.) unsalted butter, diced
1 tbsp. milk
1 2/3 cups (7 oz.) confectioners' sugar

TO DECORATE

15 pecan halves
Red, white, and blue sugar balls

MAKES 15

1. Preheat the oven to 350°F. Line two 12-cup muffin pans with 15 paper baking cups.

2. To make the cupcakes, beat the butter and sugar together until soft and creamy. Gradually beat in the eggs, a little at a time, adding a little of the flour to prevent the mixture from curdling. Stir in the rest of the flour and the ginger. Finally, mix in the cranberries, pecans, and milk.

3. Spoon the mixture into the paper baking cups and bake for 20–25 minutes or until the cupcakes are golden brown and springy to the touch. Cool in the muffin pan for 10 minutes before lifting out onto a wire rack to cool completely.

4. To make the frosting, heat the maple syrup, butter, and milk together in a small pan over a low heat (or in a bowl in the microwave for about 1 minute on full power). Sift in the confectioners' sugar and stir until you have a smooth frosting. Let cool, then beat with a wooden spoon until thick.

5. Spread the frosting over the cupcakes. Top each one with a pecan half and a scattering of red, white, and blue sugar sprinkles.

Anyone who is not keen on rich fruitcake will enjoy one—at least—of these alternative little Christmas treats instead.

Chocolate, Brandy, and Chestnut Cupcakes

1. Preheat the oven to 350°F. Line a 12-cup muffin pan with 10 paper baking cups.

2. To make the cupcakes, beat the butter and chestnut purée together until smooth, then beat in the sugar until combined. Mix in the egg yolks one at a time, then stir in the milk and melted chocolate.

3. Whisk the egg whites in a separate bowl until firm peaks form. Stir 1 tablespoon of egg white into the mixture to loosen it, before gently folding in the rest with a large metal spoon. Spoon the batter into the paper cases.

4. Bake for 20–25 minutes or until the cupcakes feel just firm to the touch. Cool in the pan for 10 minutes before lifting out onto a wire rack to cool completely.

5. To make the frosting, beat the butter until soft, then gradually beat in the sugars. Finally, beat in the brandy a teaspoon at a time. Chill the frosting in the fridge for a couple of hours to firm, if necessary.

6. Spread or pipe the frosting over the cupcakes and decorate with holly leaves piped with chocolate decorating icing and berries piped with red decorating icing. Sift over a light dusting of cocoa powder.

CUPCAKES

5 tbsp. (2½ oz.) unsalted butter, softened
¾ cup (7 oz.) chestnut purée
2 tbsp. light brown sugar
3 large eggs, separated
1 tbsp. milk
4 oz. dark chocolate, melted and cooled

BRANDY BUTTER FROSTING

6 tbsp. (3 oz.) unsalted butter, softened
1/3 cup (3 oz.) light brown sugar
2/3 cup (3 oz.) confectioners' sugar
1 tbsp. brandy

TO DECORATE

Holly leaves and berries piped with chocolate-flavored icing and red decorating icing
Cocoa powder, to dust

MAKES 10

Light and citrusy with a nutty crust, these melt-in-the-mouth cupcakes will appeal to anyone who finds buttercream and other frostings a little on the sweet side.

Spiced Honey and Lemon Drizzle Cupcakes

CUPCAKES

Scant 1 2/3 cups (7 oz.) all-purpose flour
2 tsp. baking powder
1 tsp. ground cinnamon
9 tbsp. (4½ oz.) unsalted butter, softened
Scant 1 cup (6 oz.) granulated sugar
2 tbsp. honey
Finely grated zest of 2 lemons
2 large eggs
½ cup buttermilk

TOPPING

2 tbsp. unsalted butter, softened
Scant ½ cup (2 oz.) all-purpose flour
6 tbsp. (3 oz.) granulated sugar
Scant ½ cup (2 oz.) hazelnuts, chopped
½ tsp. pumpkin pie spice
Juice of 2 lemons

MAKES 12

TIP These cupcakes are equally delicious eaten warm or cold. If eaten warm, they can be removed from their paper baking cups and topped with a generous spoonful of plain yogurt.

1. Preheat the oven to 350°F. Line a 12-cup muffin pan with paper baking cups.

2. To make the cupcakes, sift the flour, baking powder, and cinnamon into a bowl, then rub in the butter until the mixture resembles breadcrumbs. Stir in the sugar. Whisk together the honey, lemon zest, eggs, and buttermilk, and stir into the flour mixture until evenly combined. Transfer the mixture to a large pitcher and pour the batter into the paper baking cups.

3. To make the topping, rub the butter into the flour, then stir in 1 tablespoon of the sugar and the hazelnuts. Spoon the topping over the batter in the paper baking cups in an even layer.

4. Bake the cupcakes for 20 minutes or until a toothpick pushed into the center of one comes out clean. While the cupcakes are baking, mix the remaining sugar from the topping ingredients with the pumpkin pie spice and lemon juice. Spoon this mixture over the cupcakes as soon as they come out of the oven.

5. Let the cupcakes cool in the pan for 10 minutes before transferring to a wire rack to cool completely.

The secret to success here is the dark chocolate and lemon flavor combination. If you're feeling secretive (or short of time!), top the cupcakes with store-bought mini-meringues. No one need know!

Lemon Meringue Cupcakes

1. To make the meringues, preheat the oven to 225°F. Line a baking sheet with nonstick baking parchment. In a clean, grease-free bowl, whisk the egg whites to soft peaks. Add the sugar, 1 teaspoon at a time, whisking until the egg whites are stiff and shiny.

2. Spoon or pipe the mixture into 10 small mounds or rosettes on the baking sheet and bake for 1½ hours or until crisp and dry. Leave to cool on the sheet. Drizzle or pipe the melted chocolate over and let set before removing from the sheet.

3. To make the cupcakes, preheat the oven to 350°F. Line a 12-cup muffin pan with 10 paper baking cups.

4. Beat the butter and sugar together until pale and creamy. Gradually beat in the eggs, adding a little of the flour to prevent the mixture from curdling. Stir in the rest of the flour and the milk. Finally, stir in 2 tablespoons of the lemon curd.

5. Divide the mixture between the paper baking cups and bake for 20–25 minutes or until golden brown. Cool in the pan for 10 minutes, then transfer to a wire rack to cool completely.

6. Cut a wedge out of the top of each cupcake and remove. Spoon the remaining lemon curd into the hole and gently press the cake wedges on top. Place a meringue and a lemon jelly candy on each. Dust with confectioners' sugar.

MERINGUES

2 egg whites
Generous ½ cup (4 oz.) granulated sugar
2 oz. dark chocolate, melted

CUPCAKES

12 tbsp. (6 oz.) unsalted butter, softened
½ cup (4 oz.) granulated sugar
3 large eggs, beaten
Scant 2 cups (8 oz.) self-rising flour
1 tbsp. milk
6 tbsp. lemon curd

TO DECORATE

12 lemon jelly candies
Confectioners' sugar, to dust

MAKES 10

Cola adds the "wow" factor to these cupcakes. While the cocoa ensures the cola flavor isn't overpowering, they'll certainly be a talking point if you produce a plate of them for guests.

Chocolate Cola Cupcakes

CUPCAKES
Scant 1½ cups (6 oz.) self-rising flour
2 tbsp. cocoa powder
1 cup (7 oz.) light brown sugar
1 large egg
1 tsp. vanilla extract
2 tbsp. milk
12 tbsp. (6 oz.) unsalted butter
2/3 cup (5 fl. oz.) cola

CHOCOLATE COLA FROSTING
1 tbsp. (½ oz.) unsalted butter
2 tbsp. cola
1 tbsp. cocoa powder
1 2/3 cups (7 oz.) confectioners' sugar

TO DECORATE
Chocolate sprinkles
12 fizzy candies

MAKES 12

1. Preheat the oven to 350°F. Line a 12-cup muffin pan with large baking cups.

2. To make the cupcakes, sift the flour and cocoa powder into a bowl and stir in the sugar. Beat together the egg, vanilla, and milk. Melt the butter with the cola in a saucepan over a low heat, then add to the dry ingredients, stirring until mixed. Add the egg and vanilla mixture and beat well to combine.

3. Transfer the batter to a large pitcher and pour into the paper baking cups. Bake for 20–25 minutes or until a toothpick pushed into one of the cupcakes comes out clean. Cool in the pan for 10 minutes before lifting out onto a wire rack to cool completely.

4. To make the chocolate cola frosting, put the butter, cola, and cocoa powder in a small saucepan and heat gently until the butter has melted. Remove from the heat and sift in the confectioners' sugar, beating to make a smooth frosting.

5. When the cupcakes come out of the oven, spoon the frosting over them and top with chocolate sprinkles and fizzy candies. Leave until the frosting has set before removing the cupcakes from the pan.

If carrot cake is one of your favorites, you'll find these cupcakes irresistible. Make sure the carrots are grated as finely as possible before adding them to the mix.

Carrot and Golden Raisin Cupcakes

1. Preheat the oven to 350°F. Line a 12-cup muffin pan with paper baking cups.

2. To make the cupcakes, whisk the oil, sugar, eggs, and lemon zest together in a large pitcher. Sift the flour and pumpkin pie spice into a mixing bowl and pour in the egg mixture, stirring until evenly combined.

3. Stir in the carrots and golden raisins, then spoon the mixture into the paper baking cups and bake for 25–30 minutes or until the cupcakes feel firm to the touch. Let cool in the muffin pan for 10 minutes before transferring to a wire rack to cool completely.

4. To make the cream cheese frosting, beat the cream cheese until smooth. Gradually whisk in the butter before sifting in the confectioners' sugar a little at a time. Whisk well after each addition.

5. Spread the frosting over the cupcakes and top with baby carrots, molded from orange gum paste or marzipan with green molded tops.

CUPCAKES
Scant 2/3 cup sunflower oil
Scant 1 cup (6 oz.) light brown sugar
2 large eggs
Finely grated zest of 1 lemon
Scant 1½ cups (6 oz.) self-rising flour
1 tsp. pumpkin pie spice
½ lb. (7 oz.) grated carrots
¾ cup (4 oz.) golden raisins

CREAM CHEESE FROSTING
4 oz. full-fat cream cheese
4 tbsp. (2 oz.) unsalted butter, softened
1¾ cups (8 oz.) confectioners' sugar

TO DECORATE
Carrots molded from orange and green gum
    paste or marzipan

MAKES 12

TIP Make sure the cream cheese and butter are beaten together thoroughly before you start adding the confectioners' sugar or it will be difficult to achieve a smooth, creamy icing.

The chopped apricots in the mix and rich coconut milk in the frosting give these light little sponges a taste of paradise. Perfect paired with a cup of refreshing lemon tea.

Creamy Coconut and Apricot Cupcakes

CUPCAKES

½ cup (4 oz.) unsalted butter, softened
½ cup (4 oz.) light brown sugar
2 large eggs, beaten
Generous 1 cup (4 oz.) self-rising flour
1½ oz. shredded unsweetened coconut
3 oz. canned or fresh apricots, chopped into small pieces (see Tip)
1½ tbsp. coconut milk

COCONUT FROSTING

Scant 6 tbsp. (3 oz.) unsalted butter, softened
1½ cups (6 oz.) confectioners' sugar
1½ tbsp. coconut milk

TO DECORATE

Orange sugar sprinkles
Shredded unsweetened coconut, lightly toasted

MAKES 12

TIP Fresh or canned apricots are both fine for this recipe, but if using canned, pick those in natural juice rather than syrup and blot the apricots dry with paper towel before chopping.

1. Preheat the oven to 350°F. Line a 12-cup muffin pan with paper baking cups.

2. To make the cupcakes, beat the butter and sugar together until creamy. Gradually beat in the eggs, a little at a time, adding a tablespoon of the flour to prevent the mixture from curdling. Stir in the rest of the flour, the coconut, apricots, and coconut milk until evenly combined.

3. Spoon the mixture into the paper baking cups and bake for 15–20 minutes or until a toothpick pushed into the center of one of the cupcakes comes out clean. Cool in the muffin pan for 10 minutes before transferring to a wire rack to cool completely.

4. To make the frosting, beat the butter until creamy. Gradually sift in the confectioners' sugar, beating well after each addition. Stir in the coconut milk and pipe or spread over the cupcakes. Decorate with orange sugar sprinkles and a small amount of lightly toasted shredded coconut.

The classic combination of bittersweet chocolate and fragrant peppermint combine perfectly to make these colorful two-tone cakes.

Chocolate and Peppermint Cupcakes

1. Preheat the oven to 350°F. Line a 12-cup muffin pan with paper baking cups.

2. To make the cupcakes, beat the butter and sugar together until creamy. Beat in the eggs, a little at a time, adding a tablespoon of the flour to prevent the mixture from curdling. When all the egg has been added, stir in the remaining flour.

3. Spoon half the mixture into a separate bowl. Stir the dissolved cocoa powder into one bowl and the peppermint extract, green food coloring, and milk into the other.

4. Spoon the two mixtures alternately into the paper baking cups and swirl together with a skewer or toothpick. Bake for 20 minutes or until a toothpick pushed into the center of one of the cupcakes comes out clean. Cool in the muffin pan for 10 minutes before transferring to a wire rack to cool completely.

5. To make the frosting, whisk together the mascarpone, confectioners' sugar, and butter until smooth. Add a few drops of peppermint extract and tint the frosting with green food coloring. Spread or pipe the frosting over the cupcakes.

6. Spoon the melted chocolate into a small paper piping bag and drizzle over the cupcakes. Scatter chocolate sprinkles over the top and let the chocolate set.

CUPCAKES

12 tbsp. (6 oz.) unsalted butter, softened
Scant 1 cup (6 oz.) granulated sugar
3 large eggs, beaten
Scant 1½ cups (6 oz.) self-rising flour
2 tbsp. cocoa powder dissolved in 1 tbsp. hot water
Few drops of peppermint extract and green food coloring
1 tbsp. milk

PEPPERMINT MASCARPONE FROSTING

3 oz. mascarpone
2¾ cups confectioners' sugar
6 tbsp. (2 oz.) unsalted butter, softened
Few drops of peppermint extract and green food coloring

TO DECORATE

2 oz. dark chocolate, melted
Chocolate sprinkles

MAKES 12

TIP Food colorings are very concentrated, so only add the green coloring a few drops at a time. You can always you can't take it out!

These are not the classic butterfly cupcakes but fun cakes with butterflies on top; albeit edible ones made from rice paper and brightly colored icing.

Butterfly Cupcakes with Pineapple and Cream

CUPCAKES

3 oz. pineapple (fresh or canned in juice),
   chopped into small pieces
Scant 2 cups (8 oz.) self-rising flour
5 tbsp. (2 oz.) semolina
½ cup (4 oz.) light brown sugar
Finely grated zest of 1 orange
1 large egg
2 oz. ricotta cheese
Scant ½ cup sunflower oil
1 tbsp. milk

TO DECORATE

Scant 2/3 cup (5 fl.oz.) heavy cream
Extra chopped pineapple
Orange and lemon sugar sprinkles
Butterflies cut from edible rice paper and
   piped with decorating icing (see Tip)

MAKES 10

TIP To make the butterflies, draw butterfly shapes on edible wafer paper such as rice paper and cut out with small scissors. Fold the butterfly shapes in half so they are "V" shaped and decorate with colored piped icing. Let set on crumpled foil or plastic wrap.

1. Preheat the oven to 350°F. Line a 12-cup muffin pan with 10 paper baking cups.

2. To make the cupcakes, dust the chopped pineapple in a little of the flour. Sift the rest of the flour into a mixing bowl and stir in the semolina, sugar, and orange zest.

3. Whisk together the egg, ricotta cheese, sunflower oil, and milk. Stir into the dry ingredients to make a fairly stiff mixture. Finally, mix in the flour-dusted pineapple.

4. Spoon the mixture into the paper baking cups and bake for 20–25 minutes or until golden brown and a toothpick pushed into the center of one of the cakes comes out clean. Cool in the muffin pan for 10 minutes before removing to a wire rack to cool completely.

5. To decorate, whip the cream until it holds its shape. Top the cupcakes with the whipped cream, a few pieces of chopped pineapple, orange and lemon sugar sprinkles, and butterflies cut from rice paper and piped with decorating icing.

Polenta is traditionally served as an accompaniment to an Italian meat dish. Surprisingly, its flavor comes alive when added to a citrus cupcake mix. The slightly crunchy texture crumbles less than an ordinary sponge.

Lemon and Polenta Cupcakes

CUPCAKES

14 tbsp. (7 oz.) unsalted butter, softened
1 cup (7 oz.) light brown sugar
3 large eggs, beaten
Generous 1 cup (5 oz.) all-purpose flour
Scant 1 cup (4 oz.) polenta
1½ tsp. baking powder
Finely grated zest of 2 lemons
2 tbsp. lemon juice

LEMON BUTTERCREAM

8 tbsp. (4 oz.) unsalted butter, softened
1¾ cups (8 oz.) confectioners' sugar
About 2 tbsp. lemon juice

TO DECORATE

Yellow sugar sprinkles

MAKES 12

TIP Polenta is finely ground cornmeal which is found near the pasta packages in major supermarkets. It is sometimes sold as "corn grits."

1. Preheat the oven to 350°F. Line a 12-cup muffin pan with paper baking cups.

2. To make the cupcakes, beat the butter and sugar together until pale and creamy. Beat in the eggs a little at a time, adding a tablespoon of the flour to stop the mixture from curdling.

3. Sift in the rest of the flour, add the polenta and baking powder, and stir in with the lemon zest and juice.

4. Divide the mixture between the paper baking cups and bake for 20–25 minutes or until the cupcakes are golden and a toothpick pushed into the middle of one comes out clean. Cool in the muffin pan for 10 minutes before removing to a wire rack to cool completely.

5. To make the buttercream, beat the butter until creamy and soft. Gradually sift in the confectioners' sugar a little at a time, beating well after each addition, and adding enough lemon juice to make a smooth, soft frosting.

6. Spread the buttercream over the cupcakes and decorate with yellow sugar sprinkles.

Is it a cupcake or a dessert in disguise? The answer is simple: both! These clever cakes have a creamy custard center that works perfectly with the plums. Feel free to experiment with other fruits, such as peaches or apples.

Plums and Custard Cupcakes

1. Preheat the oven to 400°F. Line a 12-cup muffin pan with paper baking cups.

2. Toss the chopped plums in the brown sugar and cinnamon, then spread out in a single layer in a shallow baking dish. Cover with foil and roast for 10 minutes. Remove the foil and roast for 5 minutes more. Cool, drain off any juices from the pan, and set aside.

3. Reduce the oven temperature to 350°F. Beat the butter and granulated sugar together until pale and creamy. Beat in the eggs one at a time, adding a tablespoon of the flour with each egg to prevent the mixture from curdling.

4. Sift in the rest of the flour and stir in with the milk and roasted plums. Divide about half of the cake batter between the paper baking cups, top with a small spoonful of custard, then cover with the rest of the batter.

5. Bake for 25 minutes or until golden brown and just firm to the touch. Cool in the pan for 10 minutes before transferring to a wire rack to cool completely.

INGREDIENTS

9 oz. plums, pitted and chopped
3 tbsp. light brown sugar
1 tsp. ground cinnamon
8 tbsp. (4 oz.) unsalted butter, softened
Generous 1 cup (4 oz.) granulated sugar
2 large eggs
Scant 1½ cups (6 oz.) self-rising flour
1 tbsp. milk
8 tbsp. thick custard, chilled (see Tip)

MAKES 12

TIP The plums need to be ripe but still firm enough so they don't fall apart when roasted in the oven. Make thick custard according to the packet instructions and you'll have plenty left over for your next dessert.

Not the devil's work, just devilishly good cupcakes that all chocoholics will love.

Devil's Food Cupcakes

1. Preheat the oven to 350°F. Line a 12-cup muffin pan with paper baking cups.

2. To make the cupcakes, mix together half the sugar, the cocoa powder, and 2/3 cup of the buttermilk and set aside for 10 minutes.

3. Beat the butter in a mixing bowl with the rest of the sugar until creamy. Gradually beat in the egg until combined, adding the vanilla with the last of the egg.

4. Sift in the flour and baking powder and stir in, followed by the remaining buttermilk. Finally, stir in the cocoa mixture. Spoon the batter into the paper baking cups.

5. Bake for about 20 minutes or until firm to the touch. Let the cupcakes cool in the pan for 10 minutes before transferring to a wire rack to cool completely.

6. To make the frosting, snip the marshmallows into small pieces with scissors, if large, and put in a saucepan with the milk. Heat gently until melted, stirring until smooth. Set aside to cool. In a clean, grease-free bowl, whisk the egg whites until soft peaks form, add the sugar, and whisk again until stiff. Very carefully fold the melted marshmallows into the egg whites until evenly mixed in and then chill in the fridge until firm enough to spread, stirring from time to time.

7. Spread the frosting (which will be very sticky) over the cupcakes with a small round-bladed knife. Decorate with chocolate sprinkles.

CUPCAKES
225 g (8 oz.) granulated sugar
50 g (2 oz.) cocoa powder
225 ml (8 fl. oz.) buttermilk
50 g (2 oz.) unsalted butter, softened
1 large egg, beaten
1 tsp vanilla extract
115 g (4 oz.) plain flour
1 tsp. baking powder

MARSHMALLOW FROSTING
150 g (5 oz.) white marshmallows
2 tbsp. milk
2 egg whites
25 g (1 oz.) superfine sugar

TO DECORATE
Chocolate sprinkles

MAKES 12

TIP If you find you have frosting left over, this can be kept in the refrigerator in a covered bowl for up to two days—a good excuse for making another batch!

Bring a taste of the tropics to any teatime table with these mango and lime-flavored cupcakes topped with a sticky passion-fruit icing.

Mango, Lime and Passion Fruit Cupcakes

CUPCAKES

¾ cup (5 oz.) light brown sugar
3 large eggs
Finely grated zest and juice of 1 lime
7 oz. ripe mango flesh, finely chopped
Scant 2 cups (8 oz.) self-rising flour

FROSTING

3 passion fruit
1¼ cups (5 oz.) confectioners' sugar
Green or yellow crystal sugar

MAKES 12

TIP Heating the passion fruit pulp and seeds makes it easier to separate them. However, if preferred, the seeds of all three fruits can be stirred directly into the confectioners' sugar.

1. Preheat the oven to 350°F. Line a 12-cup muffin pan with paper baking cups.

2. Whisk the sugar, eggs, lime zest, and juice together until pale-colored and creamy. Blot the chopped mango with paper towels to remove excess juice and dust the fruit with a little of the flour.

3. Gently fold the remaining flour and the mango into the mixture until evenly combined. Let the mixture stand for 10 minutes to allow it to thicken a little before spooning into the paper baking cups. Bake for 15–20 minutes or until springy to the touch and golden brown.

4. Cool in the muffin pan for 10 minutes before transferring to a wire rack to cool completely.

5. To make the frosting, cut the passion fruit in half. Scoop out the pulp and seeds of one fruit and stir these into the confectioners' sugar. Scoop out the pulp and seeds from the other two fruit into a small bowl and heat in the microwave for 45 seconds on full power. Push through a sieve to remove the seeds, then stir the pulp into the confectioners' sugar.

6. Spoon the frosting over the cupcakes and top with a light sprinkling of pale green or yellow crystal sugar.

Made with whole-grain flour and sweetened with applesauce and brown sugar, you can feel a little less guilty about indulging in one of these gorgeous cupcakes. If applesauce isn't available, use freshly cooked apple, finely chopped and simmered with a little lemon juice until soft.

Apple Sauce and Cinnamon Cupcakes

1. Preheat the oven to 350°F. Line a 12-cup muffin pan with paper baking cups.

2. To make the cupcakes, beat the butter and brown sugar together until smooth and creamy. Gradually beat in the eggs, a little a time, adding a spoonful of the flour to prevent the mixture from curdling.

3. Stir in the rest of the flour, the cinnamon, and the applesauce. Spoon the mixture into the paper baking cups and decorate by sprinkling a little pearl sugar on top of each cupcake.

4. Bake for 20–25 minutes or until a toothpick pushed into the center of one of the cupcakes comes out clean. Cool in the pan for 10 minutes before transferring to a wire rack to cool completely.

CUPCAKES

12 tbsp. (6 oz.) unsalted butter, softened
Scant 1 cup (6 oz.) light brown sugar
3 large eggs, beaten
Scant 2 cups (8 oz.) whole-grain self-rising flour
1 tsp. ground cinnamon
5 tbsp. chunky applesauce

TO DECORATE

2 tbsp. pearl sugar

MAKES 12

TIP Pearl sugar, a large crystal sugar, may not be easily found in your supermarket. You can try to order it online or make your own by simply crushing a few sugar cubes with a large heavy knife.

Tangy with lemon and crunchy with black poppy seeds, these pretty, speckled cupcakes taste as good as they look.

Lemon and Poppy Seed Cupcakes

CUPCAKES

1 cup (4 oz.) ground almonds

Scant 1 cup (6 oz.) granulated sugar

2 medium egg yolks

2/3 cup (3 oz.) self-rising flour

Finely grated zest of 1 lemon

6 tbsp. (2 oz.) black poppy seeds

8 tbsp. (4 oz.) unsalted butter, melted and cooled

4 large egg whites

TO DECORATE

6 tbsp. apricot jam, warmed and strained

9 oz. yellow gum paste

White and yellow decorating icing

MAKES 12

TIP The flowers can also be made with colored gum paste. Roll out the gum paste as thinly as possible on a surface dusted with confectioners' sugar. Stamp out small flowers using a flower plunger cutter (available from cake-decorating stores). Pipe a small blob of decorating icing in the center of each flower and let it set before arranging the flowers in garlands on top of the cupcakes.

1. Preheat the oven to 350°F. Line a 12-cup muffin pan with paper baking cups.

2. To make the cupcakes, put the ground almonds, sugar, egg yolks, flour, lemon zest, and poppy seeds in a mixing bowl and stir together. Gradually drizzle in the melted butter, folding in gently until just blended. In another bowl, whisk the egg whites until they stand in soft peaks. Stir 1 tablespoon of the egg whites into the lemon and poppy seed mixture to soften, before carefully folding in the rest with a large metal spoon.

3 . Spoon the mixture into the paper baking cups and bake for 20 minutes or until a toothpick pushed into the center of a cupcake comes out clean. Cool the cupcakes in the pan for 10 minutes before transferring them to a wire rack to cool completely.

4. To decorate, brush the apricot jam over the cupcakes and cover with rounds of thinly rolled out yellow gum paste. Mark a pattern in the gum paste with the back of a knife and pipe rings of small flowers on top of each cupcake with yellow and white decorating icing. Let the icing set before serving.

A modern twist on the much-loved Black Forest Gateau, the classic recipe from the 1960s. As they are topped with fresh cream, keep the cupcakes in the refrigerator until you are ready to serve.

Black Forest Cupcakes

1. Preheat the oven to 350°F. Line a 12-cup muffin pan with large paper baking cups.

2. To make the cupcakes, beat the butter and brown sugar together until creamy. Gradually beat in the eggs, adding a little of the flour to prevent the mixture from curdling. Stir in the remaining flour, melted dark chocolate, and milk until evenly combined. Finally, stir in the cherry jam.

3. Spoon the mixture into the paper baking cups and bake for 20–25 minutes or until a toothpick pushed into the center of one of the cupcakes comes out clean. Cool in the muffin pan for 10 minutes before transferring to a wire rack to cool completely.

4. To decorate, cut a small piece out of the top of each cupcake and fill the hole with cherry jam. Trim the bases of the pieces of cake you have cut out, then place them on top of the jam.

5. Whip the cream and kirsch (if using) together until the cream holds its shape. Pipe or spread the cream over the top of the cupcakes, decorate with chocolate sprinkles and top each one with a fresh cherry.

CUPCAKES

12 tbsp. (6 oz.) unsalted butter, softened
1¼ cups (5 oz.) dark brown sugar
2 large eggs, beaten
Scant 2 cups (8 oz.) self-rising flour
4 oz. dark chocolate, melted
2 tbsp. milk
2 tbsp. cherry jam

TO DECORATE

2 tbsp. cherry jam
Scant 2/3 cup (5 fl.oz.) heavy cream
2 tbsp. kirsch (optional)
2–3 tbsp. chocolate sprinkles
12 fresh black cherries

MAKES 12

TIP The crystals of dark and light brown sugar can clump together, even when the sugar is soft, so before adding it to a recipe, break up any lumps with your fingers or the back of a spoon so it mixes in evenly with the other ingredients.

In the cupcake world, these are "healthy options." As a dessert, they could be eaten straight from the oven with a spoonful of natural Greek yogurt. Let them cool and enjoy them solo for breakfast with a cup of piping-hot tea or coffee.

Tangerine, Granola and Maple Syrup Cupcakes

1. Preheat the oven to 350°F. Line a 12-cup muffin pan with paper baking cups.

2. Beat the butter and sugar together until creamy. Stir in the maple syrup and then beat in the eggs a little at a time, adding a tablespoon of the flour to prevent the mixture from curdling.

3. Sift in the rest of the flour and stir in with the tangerine or orange juice, yogurt, and granola.

4. Spoon the mixture into the paper baking cups and bake for 20–25 minutes or until firm to the touch and a toothpick pushed into the center of one of the cupcakes comes out clean. Cool in the muffin pan for 10 minutes before lifting out onto a wire rack. Eat the cupcakes warm or cold with extra plain yogurt.

CUPCAKES

8 tbsp. (4 oz.) unsalted butter, softened
Generous ½ cup (4½ oz.) light brown sugar
2 tbsp. maple syrup
2 large eggs, beaten
Scant 2 cups (8 oz.) self-rising flour
4 tbsp. tangerine or orange juice
4 tbsp. plain yogurt
6 oz. granola

TO SERVE
Plain yogurt

MAKES 12

TIP Remove or break up any large pieces of the granola before adding it to the cupcake batter.

Coffee-lovers can get their extra hit of caffeine by accompanying their morning coffee with one of these stylish cupcakes. The creamy white frosting will keep chocaholics buzzing too.

Caffe Latte Cupcakes

CUPCAKES

1 tsp. cocoa powder
1 tbsp. instant coffee granules
12 tbsp. (6 oz.) unsalted butter, softened
Scant 1 cup (6 oz.) light brown sugar
3 large eggs
Scant 1½ cups (6 oz.) self-rising flour
1 tsp. baking powder

WHITE CHOCOLATE FROSTING

3 oz. white chocolate chips
Scant 3 tbsp. (1½ oz.) unsalted butter
2 tbsp. milk
1 cup (4 oz.) confectioners' sugar

TO DECORATE

4 tbsp. chocolate sprinkles
Cocoa powder, to dust

MAKES 12

1. Preheat the oven to 350°F. Line a 12-cup muffin pan with large paper baking cups.

2. To make the cupcakes, mix together the cocoa powder and coffee granules and stir in 2 tablespoons of hot water until smooth. Put the butter, brown sugar, eggs, flour, and baking powder in a bowl. Add the dissolved cocoa and coffee and whisk or beat all the ingredients together until smooth.

3. Spoon the mixture into the paper baking cups and bake for 15–20 minutes or until well risen and springy to the touch. Cool in the muffin pan for 10 minutes before lifting the cupcakes onto a wire rack to cool completely.

4. To make the frosting, melt the chocolate and butter in a bowl set over a pan of simmering water. Stir in the milk until smooth, then remove the bowl to the work surface and sift in the confectioners' sugar. Beat the icing until smooth and then spread over the cupcakes. Decorate with the chocolate sprinkles and a dusting of sifted cocoa powder.

Chocolate, nuts, and salted caramel together are a combination made in heaven. These cupcakes would be perfect for a teenage party. They'd disappear pretty quickly at a party for grown-ups too!

Salted Caramel Cupcakes

1. Preheat the oven to 350°F. Line a 12-cup muffin pan with paper baking cups.

2. To make the cupcakes, beat the butter until creamy, then gradually beat in the sugar. Gradually beat in the eggs, adding a tablespoon of the flour to prevent the mixture curdling. Stir in the remaining flour with the chocolate and pecans.

3. Spoon the mixture into the paper baking cups and bake for 20 minutes or until springy to the touch. Cool in the pan for 10 minutes before removing to a wire rack to cool completely.

4. To make the frosting, put the sugar in a small saucepan with the water and heat gently until the sugar dissolves, stirring once or twice. Bring to a boil and keep boiling until the syrup caramelizes to a dark amber color. Remove from the heat and whisk in the cream a little at a time (if you add it too quickly, the caramel will set hard, then it needs re-melting on medium in the microwave, stirring every 30 seconds). Finally beat in the vanilla and salt. Let the mixture cool for 30 minutes.

5. In a bowl, beat the butter until creamy, and then beat into the cooled caramel mixture a little at a time. When all the butter has been added, let the mixture cool completely, then chill in the refrigerator until it is thick enough to spread.

6. Spread the cupcakes with the frosting and decorate with the pecans, chocolate sprinkles, and salted candies.

CUPCAKES
12 tbsp. (6 oz.) unsalted butter, softened
Scant 1 cup (6 oz.) light brown sugar
3 large eggs, beaten
Scant 1½ cups (6 oz.) self-rising flour
½ cup (3 oz.) milk chocolate chips
2 tbsp. milk
½ cup (2 oz.) chopped pecans

SALTED CARAMEL FROSTING
Scant 1 cup (6 oz.) granulated sugar
2 tbsp. water
¾ cup heavy cream
1 tsp. vanilla extract
½ tsp. sea salt (or to taste)
10 tbsp. (5 oz.) unsalted butter, softened

TO DECORATE
2 tbsp. finely chopped pecans
Chocolate curls or sprinkles
Salted caramel chocolate candies

MAKES 12

TIP How much salt you add to the frosting depends on personal taste, so it's better to make it with unsalted butter and then add as much salt as you like.

You might not believe it but beet works extremely well in cupcake recipes, especially with chocolate as the slightly sweet beet complements the cocoa perfectly. Grate the beet as finely as you can before stirring it into the batter.

Beet and Brown Sugar Cupcakes

CUPCAKES

1 2/3 cups (7 oz.) self-rising flour
1 tbsp. cocoa powder
1 tsp. pumpkin pie spice
Scant 1 cup (6 oz.) dark brown sugar
3 large eggs
1¼ cups sunflower oil
6 oz. cooked beet, peeled and grated
Finely grated zest of ½ orange

CREAM CHEESE AND ORANGE
FROSTING

4 tbsp. (2 oz.) unsalted butter, softened
4½ oz. full-fat cream cheese
1 cup (4 oz.) confectioners' sugar
Red and orange sugar sprinkles

MAKES 12

TIP If you buy the cooked beet, avoid jars of sliced or whole small beets, as these will have been pickled in vinegar.

1. Preheat the oven to 350°F. Line a 12-cup muffin pan with paper baking cups.

2. To make the cupcakes, sift the flour, cocoa powder, and pumpkin pie spice into a bowl and stir in the brown sugar. Beat together the eggs and sunflower oil and slowly whisk into the dry ingredients, beating until the mixture is smooth—it will look curdled to begin with but it will come together as you continue beating. Whisk in the grated beet and orange zest.

3. Transfer the batter to a large pitcher and carefully pour it into the paper baking cups. Bake for 20 minutes or until a toothpick pushed into the center of one of the cupcakes comes out clean. Cool the cupcakes in the pan for 10 minutes, then lift out onto a wire rack to cool completely.

4. To make the frosting, beat the butter until creamy. Beat in the cream cheese until smooth, then sift in the confectioners' sugar and beat again until you have a soft frosting. Spread the frosting over the cupcakes and decorate with the red and orange sugar sprinkles.

Delicately perfumed with lavender, these fragrant cupcakes will transport you to Provence, France, where rolling fields of the purple flowers are an impressive and colorful sight.

Sour Cream and Lavender Cupcakes

CUPCAKES

1 tbsp. milk
1 tsp. fresh or ½ tsp. dried lavender flowers (see Tip)
3 large egg yolks
½ cup (4 fl. oz.) sour cream
Scant 1¼ cups (5½ oz.) self-rising flour
¾ cup (5 oz.) granulated sugar
9 tbsp. (4½ oz.) unsalted butter, cut into small pieces and softened

LAVENDER FROSTING

1½ cups (6 oz.) confectioners' sugar
1–2 tbsp. lemon juice
Few drops of violet or lavender food coloring

TO DECORATE

Fresh or dried lavender flowers
Sugar sprinkles

MAKES 12

TIP Dried lavender flowers specifically for culinary use can be found with the spice jars in larger supermarkets or bought online. If using fresh lavender, it must have been grown without being sprayed with pesticides.

1. Preheat the oven to 350°F. Line a 12-cup muffin pan with paper baking cups.

2. To make the cupcakes, put the milk in a small bowl, add the lavender, and heat in the microwave for 10–15 seconds or until the milk is hot. Set aside to infuse for 30 minutes.

3. Whisk the egg yolks with 2 tablespoons of the sour cream until combined. Sift the flour into a mixing bowl, then stir in the sugar, butter, and remaining sour cream. Whisk until just combined, then gradually whisk in the beaten eggs and sour cream and finally the lavender and its soaking milk.

4. Transfer the mixture to a large pitcher and pour into the paper baking cups. Bake for 20 minutes until golden brown and springy to the touch. Cool in the muffin pan for 10 minutes before transferring to a wire rack to cool completely.

5. To make the lavender frosting, sift the confectioners' sugar into a bowl and stir in enough lemon juice to give a smooth icing that coats the back of the spoon. Top the cupcakes with the frosting and decorate with a few lavender flowers and sugar sprinkles.

Porridge oats give these cupcakes a pleasantly nutty texture and flavor. Full of good things, these cupcakes are almost good for you!

Apple, Oat, and Raisin Cupcakes

1. Preheat the oven to 350°F. Line a 12-cup muffin pan with paper baking cups.

2. Peel, core, and finely chop or grate the apples. Beat the butter in a mixing bowl until creamy and then gradually beat in the brown sugar until combined.

3. Sift the flour, baking powder, and cinnamon together and add to the creamed mixture alternately with the eggs, stirring well after each addition.

4. Stir in the oats, raisins, and prepared apples, and add enough milk to make a soft mixture. Spoon into the paper baking cups and bake for 25 minutes or until a toothpick pushed into one of the cupcakes comes out clean.

5. Cool in the pan for 10 minutes before lifting out the cupcakes onto a wire rack. Serve warm or cold and dusted with confectioners' sugar.

CUPCAKES

6 oz. tart eating apples, such as Granny Smith
8 tbsp. (4 oz.) unsalted butter, softened
½ cup (4 oz.) light brown sugar
1 1/3 cups (6 oz.) all-purpose flour
1½ tsp. baking powder
1 tsp. ground cinnamon
2 large eggs, beaten
1/3 cup (2 oz.) oats
1/3 cup (2 oz.) raisins
2 tbsp. milk
Confectioners' sugar, to dust

MAKES 12

TIP The cupcakes can be made using other fruits such as apricots, plums, pears, or peaches instead of apples.

Sweet potato cupcakes are a family favorite in southern states of America. The orange-fleshed potatoes make deliciously light cakes.

Sweet Potato and Orange Cupcakes

1. Preheat the oven to 350°F. Line two 12-cup muffin pans with 18 paper baking cups.

2. To make the cupcakes, beat the butter until creamy and then gradually beat in the sugar. Beat in the eggs, a little at a time, adding a couple of tablespoons of the flour to prevent the mixture from curdling. Stir in the rest of the flour, the mashed sweet potato, orange zest, sour cream, and milk.

3. Divide the mixture between the paper baking cups and bake for 20–25 minutes or until a toothpick inserted into the center of one of the cupcakes comes out clean. Cool in the pan for 10 minutes before transferring the cupcakes to a wire rack to cool completely.

4. To make the frosting, sift the confectioners' sugar into a bowl and stir in the orange juice. Spread or drizzle over the cupcakes and decorate with sliced almonds and orange and lemon sugar sprinkles.

CUPCAKES

12 tbsp. (6 oz.) unsalted butter, softened
Scant 1 cup (6 oz.) granulated sugar
2 large eggs, beaten
Generous 2 cups (8 oz.) self-rising flour
½ lb. steamed sweet potatoes, mashed and cooled (about 2 medium, unpeeled weight)
Finely grated zest of 1 medium-large orange
4 tbsp. sour cream
2 tbsp. milk

ORANGE FROSTING

1 2/3 cups (7 oz.) confectioners' sugar
2–3 tbsp. orange juice

TO DECORATE

4 tbsp. sliced almonds
Orange and lemon sugar sprinkles

MAKES 18

If you feel like spoiling yourself after a hard day, put your feet up and take a bite out of one of these completely indulgent cupcakes—instant therapy!

Malted Chocolate Fudge Cupcakes

CUPCAKES

1¼ cup (6 oz.) all-purpose flour
6¼ tbsp. (1 oz.) malted milk powder
2 tsp. baking powder
¾ cup (2 oz.) cocoa powder
¾ cup (2 oz.) ground almonds
12 tbsp. (6 oz.) unsalted butter, softened
Scant 1 cup (6 oz.) light brown sugar
2 large eggs, beaten
2–3 tbsp. milk

CHOCOLATE FROSTING

1 cup (4 oz.) confectioners' sugar
Scant ½ cup (1½ oz.) cocoa powder
4 tbsp. (2 oz.) unsalted butter, cut into
     small pieces
1/3 cup (3 oz.) dark brown sugar
2 tbsp. water

TO DECORATE

Chocolate malt balls like Maltesers or
     Whoppers
White chocolate sprinkles or shapes

MAKES 12

1. Preheat the oven to 350°F. Line a 12-cup muffin pan with paper baking cups.

2. To make the cupcakes, sift together the flour, malted milk powder, baking powder, and cocoa powder. Mix in the ground almonds.

3. In a mixing bowl, beat the butter until creamy. Gradually beat in the brown sugar and then add the eggs, a little at a time. Beat well between each addition and add a tablespoon of the mixed dry ingredients to prevent the mixture from curdling. Stir in the remaining dry ingredients with enough milk for a soft mixture.

4. Spoon the mixture into the paper baking cups and bake for 20–25 minutes until a toothpick pushed into the center of one of the cupcakes comes out clean. Cool in the muffin pan for 10 minutes before lifting out onto a wire rack to cool completely.

5. To make the frosting, sift the confectioners' sugar and cocoa powder into a bowl. Heat the butter and brown sugar together with 2 tablespoons of the water over a low heat until the butter and sugar melt. Bring just to a boil, remove from the heat, and pour onto the confectioners' sugar and cocoa. Beat or whisk until smooth. Set aside to cool, stirring occasionally, until the frosting is thick enough to spread over the top of the cupcakes. Decorate with chocolate malt balls and white chocolate sprinkles or shapes.

If you like the all-American flavor combination then these cupcakes are for you. They can be topped with shelled or chocolate-coated peanuts.

Peanut Butter and Jelly Cupcakes

1. Preheat the oven to 350°F. Line a 12-cup muffin pan with paper baking cups.

2. To make the cupcakes, beat together the butter and sugar until creamy. Stir in the honey, then beat in the eggs a little at a time, adding a tablespoon of the flour to prevent the mixture from curdling. Fold in the rest of the flour and the milk. Finally, stir in the raspberry jam so it is not completely incorporated but forms streaks through the mixture.

3. Spoon into the paper baking cups and bake for 20 minutes or until golden brown and springy to the touch. Cool in the pan for 10 minutes before transferring the cupcakes to a wire rack to cool completely.

4. To make the frosting, beat the butter until creamy, then beat in the confectioners' sugar and peanut butter, adding enough milk to give a soft spreadable frosting. Spoon the frosting over the cupcakes, spreading it in an even layer, then top each cupcake with a whole peanut and dust with cocoa powder.

CUPCAKES
10 tbsp. (5 oz.) unsalted butter, softened
Generous ½ cup (4 oz.) granulated sugar
1 tbsp. honey
2 large eggs, beaten
Scant 2 cups (8 oz.) self-rising flour
2 tbsp. milk
2 tbsp. raspberry jam (seedless, if you prefer)

PEANUT BUTTER FROSTING
4 tbsp. (2 oz.) unsalted butter, softened
1 cup (4 oz.) confectioners' sugar
Scant ½ cup (3 oz.) crunchy peanut butter
2 tbsp. milk

TO DECORATE
Whole shelled peanuts, salted or unsalted
Cocoa powder, to dust

MAKES 12

TIP A few chopped salted peanuts sprinkled on the frosted cupcakes gives a pleasant sweet–savory sensation when you bite into them, but use unsalted nuts if you prefer.

Pass these little indulgences around after dinner with small cups of espresso and watch them disappear like magic!

Irish Coffee Mini Cupcakes

CUPCAKES

Scant 1 cup (4 oz.) self-rising flour

8 tbsp. (4 oz.) unsalted butter, cut into small dice and softened

½ cup (4 oz.) light brown sugar

2 large eggs, beaten

2 tbsp. cold strong black coffee

COFFEE FROSTING

5 tbsp. full-fat crème fraîche

1 tbsp. instant coffee granules

6 oz. white chocolate, chopped

2 tbsp. Bailey's or other Irish Cream liqueur

TO DECORATE

24 chocolate coffee beans or other small chocolate candies

Cocoa powder, to dust

MAKES 36

1. Preheat the oven to 350°F. Line mini-muffin pans with 36 mini paper baking cups.

2. To make the cupcakes, sift the flour into a mixing bowl. Add the butter, sugar, and eggs and beat until you have a smooth batter. Stir in the coffee.

3. Drop teaspoons of the mixture into the paper baking cups and bake for 10–12 minutes or until firm to the touch. Leave in the muffin pans for 10 minutes before transferring to a wire rack to cool completely.

4. To make the coffee frosting, put the crème fraîche, coffee granules, and chopped chocolate in a bowl. Stand the bowl over a pan of simmering water. Leave until the chocolate has melted and the coffee has dissolved, stirring until smooth. Stir in the liqueur and chill in the fridge until the icing is thick enough to spread or pipe, stirring from time to time.

5. Spread or pipe the frosting over the cupcakes, then top each one with a chocolate coffee bean. Dust lightly with a little cocoa powder just before serving.

These cupcakes are satisfying grabbed as a mid-morning snack with coffee but they're equally good—dare I say even better—served warm with custard or heavy cream for dessert.

Peach, Raspberry, and Amaretto Cupcakes

1. Preheat the oven to 350°F. Line a 12-cup muffin pan with paper baking cups.

2. To make the cupcakes, beat the butter and sugar together until creamy. Whisk the peach, eggs, and Amaretto or almond extract together with a fork. Beat the peach mixture into the creamed mixture a little at a time, stirring in a couple tablespoons of the flour if the mixture looks like it's curdling. Sift in the rest of the flour and the baking powder and stir in with the ground almonds until combined. Add enough milk to make a soft mixture and spoon into the paper cups.

3. To make the topping, mix the flour, brown sugar, and chopped almonds together. Stir in the melted butter and set aside for 10 minutes so the mixture has time to firm up a little. Spoon half the topping over the cupcakes and arrange the peach slices and raspberries on top, followed by the rest of the topping.

4. Bake for 20 minutes or until a toothpick pushed into the center of one of the cupcakes comes out clean. Cool in the pan for 10 minutes before transferring to a wire rack to cool completely.

CUPCAKES

8 tbsp. (4 oz.) unsalted butter, softened

Generous ½ cup (4 oz.) granulated sugar

2 peach halves, canned in fruit juice, drained, and puréed or finely chopped

2 large eggs

1 tbsp. Amaretto liqueur or 1 tsp. almond extract

Generous 1 cup (5 oz.) self-rising flour

½ tsp. baking powder

2/3 cup (3 oz.) ground almonds

1–2 tbsp. milk

TOPPING

A generous ½ cup (2½ oz.) all-purpose flour

3 tbsp. brown sugar

2 tbsp. chopped almonds

4 tbsp. (2 oz.) unsalted butter, melted

1 large fresh peach, pitted, and cut into 24 thin slices

24 fresh raspberries

MAKES 12

Wholesome and packed with mellow flavors, these feel-good cupcakes are perfect at any time of day— for breakfast, with coffee or afternoon tea, or as a luxurious midnight feast.

Date, Banana, and Molasses Cupcakes

CUPCAKES

1 2/3 cups (7 oz.) self-rising flour

1 tsp. ground cinnamon

¼ tsp. baking soda

1 large egg

4 tbsp. (2 oz.) light brown sugar

2 tbsp. dark molasses

3 small ripe bananas, peeled and cut into short lengths (about ¾ lb. total unpeeled weight)

4 oz. pitted dates, chopped

½ cup (2 oz.) chopped pecans

About 2 tbsp. milk

12 pecan halves

MAKES 12

TIP You needn't feel too guilty about indulging in these cupcakes as they're full of good things—bananas for potassium, pecans for vitamin E, and molasses, which not only contains iron and vitamin D, but has long been regarded as a cure for stomach upsets. The cupcakes need to be baked in non-stick paper cases or silicone cases or they will stick.

1. Preheat the oven to 350°F. Line a 12-cup muffin pan with paper baking cups.

2. Sift the flour, cinnamon, and baking soda into a mixing bowl. Blend the egg, brown sugar, molasses, and bananas together in a food processor or blender until smooth. Add to the dry ingredients and mix in thoroughly.

3. Finally, stir in the dates and pecans and enough cold milk to make a soft mixture that drops from the spoon when lifted.

4. Spoon the mixture into the paper baking cups, top with the pecan halves, and bake for 20–25 minutes or until a toothpick pushed into one of the cupcakes comes out clean. Cool in the muffin pan for 10 minutes before transferring to a wire rack to cool completely.

If anyone in your family is lactose-intolerant and often misses out on cakes, these cupcakes could be easily adapted into an unexpected treat by replacing the Greek yogurt with soy yogurt.

Chocolate, Walnut, and Yogurt Cupcakes

1. Preheat the oven to 350°F. Line a 12-cup muffin pan with paper baking cups.

2. To make the cupcakes, whisk together the eggs, sunflower oil, yogurt, honey, and sugar until evenly combined. Sift in the flour, baking powder, and cocoa powder, and stir in with the walnuts.

3. Spoon into the paper cases and bake for about 25 minutes or until a toothpick pushed into the center of one of the cupcakes comes out clean. Cool in the muffin pan for 10 minutes before removing the cupcakes to a wire rack to cool completely.

4. To make the frosting, melt the chocolate in a bowl over a pan of simmering water. Stir until smooth, then remove the bowl from the heat. Beat in the sugar until dissolved, followed by the yogurt. Leave to cool and thicken.

5. Pipe or spread the frosting over the cupcakes and top with the walnut halves.

CUPCAKES
3 large eggs
½ cup plus 2 tbsp. sunflower oil
5 oz. plain yogurt
4 tbsp. honey
⅓ cup (3 oz.) dark brown sugar
Scant 2 cups (8 oz.) all-purpose flour
2 tsp. baking powder
½ cup (2 oz.) cocoa powder
½ cup (2 oz.) chopped walnuts

CHOCOLATE YOGURT FROSTING
6 oz. dark chocolate, chopped
2 tbsp. dark brown sugar
5 oz. plain yogurt

TO DECORATE
12 walnut halves

MAKES 12

TIP Instead of walnuts, the cupcakes could be made and decorated with pecans or almonds.

These rose-topped cakes look beautiful layered on a cupcake stand as a modern alternative to the traditional wedding cake. Vary the shade of the frosting and roses to match the bride's color scheme.

Strawberry, White Chocolate, and Pistachio Cupcakes

CUPCAKES

8 tbsp. (4 oz.) unsalted butter, softened
Generous ½ cup (4 oz.) granulated sugar
2 large eggs, beaten
Scant 1 cup (4 oz.) self-rising flour
1 cup (6 oz.) strawberries, hulled and
   chopped
Generous 2/3 cup (3 oz.) all-purpose flour
3 tbsp. milk

CHOCOLATE AND PISTACHIO FROSTING

5 oz. white chocolate, chopped
Scant 2/3 cup (5 fl.oz.) heavy cream
1 tbsp. grenadine syrup or a few drops of
   pink food coloring

TO DECORATE

12 small icing or marzipan roses
2 tbsp. chopped pistachios

MAKES 12

TIP If making these for a wedding, it's a good idea to use a selection of different-sized paper cups. Work out the number of cakes you need and adjust the ratio of ingredients accordingly so you have enough for at least one cake per person.

1. Preheat the oven to 350°F. Line a 12-cup muffin pan with paper baking cups.

2. To make the cupcakes, beat the butter and sugar together until creamy. Gradually beat in the eggs, adding a tablespoon of the self-rising flour to prevent the mixture from curdling.

3. Dust the chopped strawberries with a little more of the self-rising flour and stir into the creamed mixture. Sift in the remaining self-rising flour and the all-purpose flour, and stir in with the milk until evenly mixed. Let stand for 10 minutes so the mixture thickens a little.

4. Spoon the batter into the paper baking cups and bake for 20–25 minutes or until a toothpick pushed into the center of one of the cupcakes comes out clean. Cool in the pan for 10 minutes, then transfer to a wire rack to cool completely.

5. To make the frosting, melt the white chocolate in a bowl over a pan of simmering water, stirring until smooth. Remove the bowl from the heat and gradually stir in the cream and grenadine (or a few drops of pink food coloring). Leave in a cool place until the icing is thick enough to spread.

6. Spread the frosting over the cupcakes, top each one with a small icing or marzipan rose, and scatter the pistachios over the top.

The crunchy topping on these dark and satisfying cupcakes makes a pleasant change from the familiar swirl of soft frosting on many cupcakes. Chopped prunes give the cakes a moist, mellow texture and flavor.

Chocolate Streusel Cupcakes

1. Preheat the oven to 350°F. Line a 12-cup muffin pan with paper baking cups.

2. To make the cupcakes, put the chopped prunes in a small bowl and pour the hot tea over them. Let stand for 30 minutes. Melt the chocolate and butter together in a bowl over a pan of simmering water, stirring until smooth. Set aside to cool.

3. Sift the flour, baking powder, and baking soda into a mixing bowl. Stir in the brown sugar, breaking up any lumps of sugar with your fingers or the back of the spoon. Whisk together the egg, milk, and vanilla and beat into the dry ingredients with the prunes, their soaking liquid, and the melted chocolate.

4. Spoon the mixture into the paper baking cups, then make the streusel topping. Rub the butter into the flour and then stir in the cocoa powder, brown sugar, and hazelnuts. Spoon the streusel mixture over the cupcakes, pressing it down lightly, and bake for 20 minutes or until a toothpick pushed into the center of one of the cupcakes comes out clean.

5. Cool in the muffin pan for 10 minutes before removing to a wire rack to cool completely.

CUPCAKES
5 oz. pitted prunes, chopped
2/3 cup (5 fl. oz.) hot tea
5 oz. dark chocolate, chopped
3 tbsp. (1½ oz.) unsalted butter
Scant 2 cups (8 oz.) all-purpose flour
1 tsp. baking powder
1 tsp. baking soda
3 tbsp. light brown sugar
1 large egg
½ cup (4 fl. oz.) milk
1 tsp. vanilla extract

STREUSEL TOPPING
4 tbsp. (2 oz.) unsalted butter
6 tbsp. all-purpose flour
1 tsp. cocoa powder
4 tbsp. light brown sugar
3 tbsp. chopped hazelnuts

MAKES 12

If breakfast is non-stop in your house, prepare these ahead. One of these banana cupcakes will be a total pick-me-up when those mid-morning hunger pangs strike. They're also perfect for popping into lunch-boxes.

Honey and Banana Cupcakes

CUPCAKES

10 tbsp. (5 oz.) unsalted butter, softened

1/3 cup (3 oz.) light brown sugar

3 tbsp. honey

½ cup (3 oz.) golden raisins

½ tsp. baking soda

2 tsp. baking powder

2½ cups (11 oz.) all-purpose flour

3 small, very ripe bananas, peeled and cut into small pieces (about ¾ lb. unpeeled weight)

2 large eggs, beaten

Scant ½ cup sunflower oil

TOPPING

2 small, firm bananas, peeled and thinly sliced

Juice of ½ lemon

2 tbsp. unsalted butter, melted

2 tbsp. crushed sugar cubes

MAKES 15

TIP If you don't have a food processor, mash the bananas with a fork and stir them into the creamed butter and sugar alternately with the flour and beaten eggs. When all the bananas, flour, and eggs have been added, gradually stir in the oil, a little at a time.

1. Preheat the oven to 325°F. Line two 12-cup muffin pans with 15 paper baking cups.

2. To make the cupcakes, beat the butter until creamy and gradually beat in the brown sugar. Stir in the honey and golden raisins. Sift together the baking soda, baking powder, and flour. Put the bananas, eggs, and sunflower oil in a food processor and blend until smooth.

3. Stir the flour and egg mixtures alternately into the creamed butter and sugar, mixing each addition into the cake batter before stirring in the next. Divide the batter between the paper baking cups.

4. For the topping, toss the banana slices in the lemon juice and arrange over the cupcakes. Brush with the melted butter, sprinkle with the crushed sugar cubes, and bake for 20–25 minutes or until a toothpick pushed into one of the cupcakes comes out clean. Cool in the muffin pan for 10 minutes before transferring to a wire rack to cool. Eat the cupcakes warm or cold.

Whoopie Pies

Whoopie Pies

A whoopie pie has everything a delicious treat should have—contrasting tastes and textures from the very first bite, an interesting or simply indulgent filling that sandwiches the two soft cookie layers, and a cheerful name. Just thinking about the name "whoopie pie" makes one smile.

The provenance of whoopie pies has become the stuff of legend. A culinary legacy from the Pennsylvania Amish communities of New England; women were said to have baked these cookie-like cakes called "hucklebucks" and popped them into lunch boxes for their farmer husbands and sons. The story has it that when lunchtime came and their menfolk opened the lids of their boxes, they cried out "whoopie" in delight. Although whoopie pies are now found all over America and in many other countries around the world, they're still considered a New England specialty and have been designated the "Official State Treat of Maine."

Traditionally made from a chocolate cake mix and later from ginger or pumpkin cake mixes, today lots of different flavored whoopie mixtures have been created. Hopefully the ones I've devised for this book will expand your existing collection of recipes or, if you're a newcomer to making whoopies, you'll be tempted to have a go.

Basic Equipment

Very little is needed to make whoopie pies beyond the usual cake-making equipment of measuring cups and pitchers, scales, bowls, sieves, and spoons.

Specialized shallow-well whoopie pie pans are now available. However, most recipes can be baked on large baking sheets lined with baking parchment.

Ingredients

The basic ingredients for whoopies are flour (usually all-purpose with a raising agent added, but self-rising flour also works well), granulated sugar, egg, butter or another fat, a flavoring—purists would say chocolate and vanilla—and a milk product. Buttermilk is traditional but sour cream or plain yogurt can also be used.

Marshmallow frosting (or 7-minute frosting as it is also known) or flavored buttercream are the traditional fillings. In this chapter I have given a whole variety of different fillings and flavors that you can mix and match to suit your own tastes. Whatever you're in the mood for – from decadent chocolate to sweet and juicy fruit – you'll find something here to keep everyone happy.

Making perfect whoopie pies

1. When making your mixture, don't over beat it when you add the dry ingredients, simply stir or fold until everything is just combined. This will stop the whoopie halves rising too much as they bake and ensure their texture stays light and airy rather than doughy and heavy.

2. If using a baking sheet lined with baking parchment rather than a whoopie pan, the mixture is likely to spread, so place spaced-out spoonfuls of the mixture on the sheet. While this can be done with a tablespoon, the quickest and easiest way is to spoon out the mixture using a small 1½–2-inch ice-cream scoop with a spring-release mechanism. A scoop will also make even shapes.

3. Once the whoopies are baked, take the sheet or pan out of the oven and neaten the edges with a knife whilst they are still soft. It's best to do this while the whoopies are still warm as they may crack if left to cool.

4. Once the edges are neatened you can leave the whoopies to cool on a wire rack. While they are cooling, whip or mix together your filling ingredients. Make sure the whoopies are completely cool before starting to sandwich the whoopie halves together.

5. When sandwiching whoopies with filling, match even-sized halves together in pairs when possible. Pipe or spread the filling over one half, topping it with the other.

6. Decorate the whoopies with confectioners' sugar, cocoa powder, frosting, nuts or edible cake decorations. Now all you have to do is eat them!

Not classic whoopies, I know, but sandwiching these crunchy Italian almond cookies with dark chocolate cream welcomes them into part of the extended "whoopie family."

Mini Amaretti and Dark Chocolate Whoopie Pies

1. Preheat the oven to 350°F. Line two baking sheets with baking parchment.

2. To make the whoopie pies, whisk the egg white, Amaretto, and almond extract lightly together with a fork. In a large mixing bowl, stir the almonds and confectioners' sugar together until thoroughly mixed. Make a well in the center of the dry ingredients, pour in the egg white and, with a fork, mash the ingredients together to make a stiff paste.

3. Divide the paste in half and shape each roll into a cylinder approximately 6 inches long. Cut each cylinder into 15 pieces and roll each piece into a loose ball with your hands. Arrange the balls on the baking sheets and bake for 15 minutes or until golden. Let cool on the baking sheets.

4. To make the filling, melt the chocolate in a bowl over a pan of simmering water, stirring until smooth. Remove from the heat and beat in the sugar until it dissolves, followed by the crème fraîche. If the crème fraîche is straight from the refrigerator, add it gradually or the filling will become too solid. If this happens, heat in the microwave for a few seconds.

5. Sandwich the amaretti halves together in pairs with the chocolate filling to make 15 tiny whoopie pies. Dust with cocoa powder before serving.

WHOOPIE PIES
1 large egg white
1 tbsp. Amaretto liqueur
¼ tsp. almond extract
Scant 2 cups (6 oz.) ground almonds
1¾ cups (8 oz.) confectioners' sugar

DARK CHOCOLATE FILLING
6 oz. dark chocolate, chopped
2 tbsp. dark brown sugar
10 tbsp. (5 fl. oz.) crème fraîche

TO DECORATE
Cocoa powder, to dust

MAKES 15

TIP Only roll the dough loosely into balls as they need to have small cracks in them to allow the air in and keep the amaretti light.

You could vary the berries you use in this delicious recipe according to preference or season. Try substituting blackberries for the blueberries and raspberries for the strawberries.

Blueberry and Strawberry Whoopie Pies

WHOOPIE PIES

4 oz. blueberries
Scant 3½ cups (12 oz.) all-purpose flour
8 tbsp. (4 oz.) unsalted butter, softened
Scant 1 cup (6 oz.) granulated sugar
1 large egg
1 tsp. baking soda
16 tbsp. (8 fl. oz.) sour cream

FILLING

14 tbsp. (7 fl. oz.) full-fat crème fraîche
6 oz. strawberries, hulled and sliced or
*   quartered*

TO DECORATE

Confectioners' sugar, to dust

MAKES 15

1. Preheat the oven to 350°F. Grease the whoopie pie pans or line three baking sheets with baking parchment.

2. To make the whoopie pies, roughly chop the blueberries and dust with a little of the flour. Beat the butter and sugar together until light and creamy. Beat in the egg until mixed in.

3. Sift in the rest of the flour with the baking soda and stir in with the blueberries and sour cream.

4. Place tablespoons of the mixture into the pans or spaced out on the baking sheets and bake for about 10 minutes or until springy to the touch. Let cool for 10 minutes, before transferring to a wire rack to cool completely.

5. To fill, fold the crème fraîche and strawberries together and use to sandwich the whoopie pies together in pairs. Sift over a light dusting of confectioners' sugar.

Chunks of chocolate in the cookie layers, and even more in the peanut butter filling, make a truly decadent combination. One just won't be enough.

Chocolate Chip and Peanut Butter Whoopie Pies

1. Preheat the oven to 350°F. Grease the whoopie pie pans or line two or three baking sheets with baking parchment.

2. To make the whoopie pies, whisk together the sugar, egg, melted butter, and milk. Sift the flour into a bowl and pour in the egg mixture, stirring until just combined. Fold in the chocolate chips.

3. Place tablespoons of the mixture in the pans or spaced out on the baking sheets to make 24 pies, and bake for 10–12 minutes or until springy to the touch. Let cool for 10 minutes before transferring to a wire rack to cool completely.

4. To make the filling, beat the peanut butter until soft, adding a little milk if necessary. Mix in the chocolate and hazelnut spread without stirring it in completely so the two mixtures are marbled. Sandwich the whoopie pies together in pairs with the filling.

WHOOPIE PIES

¾ cup (5 oz.) light brown sugar

1 large egg

8 tbsp. (4 oz.) unsalted butter, melted and cooled

½ pint (4 fl. oz.) milk

Scant 3 cups (11 oz.) self-rising flour

2 oz. milk chocolate chips

PEANUT BUTTER FILLING

9 tbsp. (5 oz.) smooth or crunchy unsalted peanut butter

1–2 tbsp. milk, if needed

8 tbsp. (4 oz.) chocolate and hazelnut spread

MAKES 12

A slightly cheeky variation on the classic whoopie pie... Hand these around at a party or serve with steaming coffee and your guests will be too busy biting into layers of crisp meringue and the coffee cream center to notice the difference.

Meringue Whoopie Kisses with Coffee Cream

MERINGUE WHOOPIES

3 large egg whites

Scant 1 cup (6 oz.) granulated sugar

DECORATION AND FILLING

2/3 cup (5 fl. oz.) heavy cream

1 tsp. instant coffee granules. dissolved in 1 tbsp. hot water and cooled

Cocoa powder, to dust

MAKES 10

TIP It's important to add the sugar to the egg whites very gradually to begin with so the whites can incorporate the sugar evenly and avoid any leaking syrup when the meringues are in the oven.

1. Preheat the oven to 225°F. Line two baking sheets with baking parchment.

2. To make the whoopie meringues, in a clean, dry bowl, whisk the egg whites until standing in soft peaks. Whisk in the granulated sugar a teaspoon at a time to begin with, and then, as the egg whites start to thicken, the sugar can be added in a steady stream.

3. Spoon or pipe 10 shallow mounds of meringue on each baking sheet and bake in the oven for 2 hours or until dry and crisp. Turn off the oven and leave them in there to cool before carefully lifting the meringues off the parchment.

4. To make the filling, whip the cream with the cooled coffee until it holds its shape and use to sandwich the meringue whoopies together in pairs. Dust with cocoa powder before serving.

These whoopie pies are totally irresistible. If you like the classic combination of chocolate and orange, you could flavor the filling with orange juice and a little finely grated zest instead of vanilla.

Chocolate and Vanilla Whoopie Pies

1. Preheat the oven to 350°F. Grease the whoopie pie pans or line two or three baking sheets with baking parchment.

2. To make the whoopie pies, beat the butter until creamy in a mixing bowl, then gradually beat in the light brown sugar. Beat in the egg and vanilla until combined. Sift together the flour, cocoa powder, and baking soda and stir into the mixture a little at a time with the buttermilk. Finally, stir in the milk.

3. Place tablespoons of the mixture in the pans or spaced out on the baking sheets to make 30 pies and bake for 10–12 minutes or until just firm to the touch. Let cool for 10 minutes before transferring to a wire rack to cool completely.

4. To make the filling, beat the butter until creamy. Gradually sift in the confectioners' sugar, beating well after each addition and adding the milk to make a smooth icing. Finally, stir in the vanilla extract.

5. Sandwich the whoopie pies together in pairs with the filling.

WHOOPIE PIES

10 tbsp. (5 oz.) unsalted butter, softened
1 cup (7 oz.) light brown sugar
1 large egg
1 tsp. vanilla extract
Scant 3 cups (11 oz.) all-purpose flour
¼ cup (2 oz.) cocoa powder
½ tsp. baking soda
10 tbsp. (5 oz.) buttermilk
2 tbsp. milk

FILLING

12 tbsp. (6 oz.) unsalted butter, softened
3 cups (12 oz.) confectioners' sugar
3 tbsp. milk
1 tsp. vanilla extract

MAKES 15

Decorated with the sunny colors of the Caribbean; savor the flavor of the infamous cocktail with every bite. If using canned pineapple, drain it well and blot with kitchen paper to remove any excess juice.

Pina Colada Whoopie Pies

WHOOPIE PIES

8 tbsp. (4 oz.) unsalted butter, softened
Scant 1 cup (6 oz.) granulated sugar
1 large egg
Scant 3 cups (11 oz.) self-rising flour
1 pineapple ring, canned or fresh, chopped into small pieces
10 fl. oz coconut milk

CREAMY RUM FILLING

8 tbsp. (4 oz.) unsalted butter, softened
1¾ cups (8 oz.) confectioners' sugar
2 tbsp. rum or pineapple juice

COCONUT FROSTING

1½ cups (6 oz.) confectioners' sugar
2 tbsp. coconut milk

TO DECORATE

Candied pineapple, cut into small pieces
Blue and yellow sugar sprinkles

MAKES 14

1. Preheat the oven to 350°F. Grease the whoopie pie pans or line two or three baking sheets with baking parchment.

2. To make the whoopie pies, cream the butter and granulated sugar together in a mixing bowl until light and fluffy. Gradually add the egg, beating well until mixed in. Sift in the flour and stir in with the pineapple and coconut milk.

3. Place tablespoons of the mixture in the pans or spaced out on the baking sheets to make 28 pies and bake for 10–12 minutes or until firm to the touch. Let cool for 10 minutes before transferring to a wire rack to cool completely.

4. To make the filling, beat the butter until creamy. Gradually sift in the confectioners' sugar, beating well after each addition. Finally, stir in the rum or pineapple juice. Sandwich the whoopie pies together in pairs with the rum filling.

5. To make the frosting, sift the confectioners' sugar into a bowl and stir in the coconut milk until smooth. Spread or drizzle over the top of the whoopie pies and decorate with the candied pineapple and blue and yellow sugar sprinkles.

WHOOPIE PIES

8 tbsp. (4 oz.) unsalted butter, softened
¾ cup (5 oz.) granulated sugar
1 tbsp. honey
1 large egg
Scant 2½ cups (10 oz.) all-purpose flour
½ tsp. baking soda
2 oz. shredded unsweetened coconut
Finely grated zest of 1 lime
10 fl. oz. sour cream

COCONUT FILLING

12 tbsp. (6 oz.) unsalted butter, softened
3 cups (12 oz.) confectioners' sugar
2 tbsp. milk
2 tbsp. grated fresh coconut

LIME FROSTING

1½ cups (6 oz.) confectioners' sugar
Juice of 1 lime
Few drops of green food coloring
   (optional)

TO DECORATE

Fresh coconut shavings
Lime zest

MAKES 15

The sharp tang of limes cuts the sweetness of these whoopies, while coconut adds a creamy smoothness. Tint the icing with a little green food coloring if you wish.

Key Lime and Coconut Whoopie Pies

1. Preheat the oven to 350°F. Grease the whoopie pie pans or line two or three baking sheets with baking parchment.

2. To make the whoopie pies, beat the butter and sugar together in a mixing bowl until light and fluffy. Beat in the honey and the egg, then sift in the flour and baking soda and stir in with the shredded coconut, lime zest, and sour cream.

3. Place tablespoons of the mixture in the trays or spaced apart on the baking sheets to make 30 pies and bake for 10–12 minutes or until springy to the touch. Let cool for 10 minutes before transferring to a wire rack to cool completely.

4. To make the filling, beat the butter until creamy. Gradually sift in the confectioners' sugar, beating well after each addition and adding the milk to make a smooth icing. Finally, stir in the grated coconut. Use to sandwich the whoopie pies together in pairs.

5. To make the frosting, sift the confectioners' sugar into a bowl and stir in enough lime juice to make a smooth frosting. Tint the frosting with a few drops of green food coloring, if liked, and drizzle or spread over the whoopies. Decorate with fresh coconut shavings and lime zest.

A fresh fruit-filled treat! Don't get carried away by how healthy you're being, as these gorgeous whoopies also contain a generous layer of thick heavy cream.

Blackberry Whoopie Pies with Apple Filling

1. Preheat the oven to 350°F. Grease the whoopie pie pans or line two or three baking sheets with baking parchment.

2. To make the whoopie pies, beat the butter and sugar together in a mixing bowl until light and creamy. Beat in the honey and then the egg until mixed in.

3. Roughly chop the blackberries and dust with a little of the flour. Sift the rest of the flour into the mixture with the cinnamon, add the milk and the blackberries, and fold everything together until evenly combined. Let the mixture stand for 10 minutes.

4. Place tablespoons of the mixture in the pans or spaced out on the baking sheets to make 24 pies and bake for about 15 minutes or until just firm to the touch. Let cool for 10 minutes before transferring to a wire rack to cool completely.

5. To make the filling, put the chopped apples in a pan and add the lemon juice. Cover the pan and cook over a low heat until the apples are soft. Set aside to cool and then drain well to remove excess liquid.

6. Sandwich the whoopie pies together in pairs with the stewed apples and whipped cream.

WHOOPIE PIES

10 tbsp. (5 oz.) unsalted butter, softened
¾ cup (5 oz.) light brown sugar
2 tbsp. honey
1 large egg
¾ cup (4 oz.) blackberries
Scant 3½ cups (12 oz.) self-rising flour
1 tsp. ground cinnamon
¾ cup (6 fl. oz.) milk

FILLING

1 lb. dessert apples, peeled, cored, and
   chopped
2 tbsp. lemon juice
Scant 1 cup (7 fl. oz.) whipped heavy cream

MAKES 12

Peaches, raspberries, and whipped vanilla cream make these whoopies perfect for summertime and long al fresco lunches. Try serving as dessert after an evening barbecue.

Peach Melba Whoopie Pies

WHOOPIE PIES
8 tbsp. (4 oz.) unsalted butter, softened
¾ cup (5 oz.) granulated sugar
1 large egg
Scant 3½ cups (12 oz.) all-purpose flour
½ pint (8 fl. oz.) sour cream
4 tbsp. milk
2 tbsp. peach jam

CREAM FILLING AND TOPPING
2/3 cup (5 fl. oz.) heavy cream
1 tsp. vanilla extract
2 fresh peaches, ripe but firm
5 oz. raspberries

TO DECORATE
Sugar sprinkles

MAKES 12

1. Preheat the oven to 350°F. Grease the whoopie pie pans or line two or three baking sheets with baking parchment.

2. To make the whoopie pies, beat the butter and sugar together in a mixing bowl until light and fluffy. Beat in the egg and then stir in the flour, sour cream, milk, and peach jam.

3. Place tablespoons of the mixture in the pans or spaced out on the baking sheets to make 24 pies and bake for 15–20 minutes or until just firm to the touch. Let cool for 10 minutes before transferring to a wire rack to cool completely.

4. To make the filling, whip the cream with the vanilla until it holds its shape. Halve the peaches and pit them. Cut the peach halves into thin slices.

5. Sandwich the whoopie pies together in pairs using three-quarters of the cream, the peach slices, and the raspberries, reserving the rest for decoration. Spoon or pipe the remaining cream on top of the whoopies and decorate with the reserved peach slices and raspberries. Top with sugar sprinkles.

Any variety of pear can be used to make these whoopies. It's important to choose one that is ripe and fragrant but still quite firm so it can be chopped or grated.

Pear and Ginger Whoopie Pies

1. Preheat the oven to 350°F. Grease the whoopie pie pans or line two or three baking sheets with baking parchment.

2. To make the whoopie pies, peel, core, and finely chop or grate the pear. Toss it with the lemon juice. Beat the butter and sugar together until light and creamy then beat in the egg. Sift in the flour and ginger and stir in with the milk. When evenly blended, stir in the pear and lemon juice.

3. Place tablespoons of the mixture into the pans or spaced out on the baking sheets to make 24 pies and bake for about 10–15 minutes or until just firm. Cool for 10 minutes, before transferring to a wire rack to cool completely.

4. To make the apricot filling, put the apricots in a pan with the jam and orange juice and simmer gently, with the pan covered, for about 20 minutes or until the apricots are very soft. Leave to cool and then blend to a purée in a blender.

5. Transfer the filling to a bowl and, if necessary, stir in cold water or extra orange juice to make a spreadable mixture. Sandwich the whoopie pies together in pairs with the apricot filling. Dust with confectioners' sugar and ground ginger before serving.

WHOOPIE PIES
1 ripe but firm pear
1 tbsp. lemon juice
10 tbsp. (5 oz.) unsalted butter, softened
¾ cup (5 oz.) granulated sugar
1 large egg
Scant 3 cups (11 oz.) self-rising flour
1 tsp. ground ginger
12 tbsp. (6 fl. oz.) milk

APRICOT FILLING
1 lb ready-to-eat dried apricots, snipped
  into small pieces
2 tbsp. apricot jam
¾ pint (6 fl. oz.) orange juice

TO DECORATE
Confectioners' sugar and ground ginger,
  to dust

MAKES 12

Red velvet cakes are a familiar sight in cupcake stores and bakeries in the U.S. The reaction of the acid in the buttermilk when it mixes with the cocoa is said to bring out a natural red color, but most recipes add red food coloring.

Red Velvet Whoopie Pies

1. Preheat the oven to 350°F. Grease the whoopie pie pans or line two or three baking sheets with baking parchment.

2. To make the whoopie pies, beat the butter and sugar together until light and fluffy. Beat in the egg until evenly combined.

3. Sift together the flour, cocoa powder, and baking soda, stirring it into the mixture alternately with the buttermilk. Finally, stir in the red food coloring.

4. Place tablespoons of the mixture in the pans or spaced out on the baking sheets to make 28 pies and bake for 10–12 minutes or until just firm to the touch. Let cool for 5 minutes before transferring to a wire rack to cool completely.

5. To make the filling, put the marshmallows in a pan with the milk. Heat gently until melted, stirring until smooth. Set aside to cool. In a clean, dry bowl, whisk the egg whites to soft peaks, add the sugar and whisk until stiff. Fold the melted marshmallows into the egg whites until evenly mixed in, then chill until firm enough to spread, stirring occasionally.

6. Sandwich the whoopies in pairs with the marshmallow filling. Any leftover filling can be stored in a covered bowl in the fridge for 1–2 days.

WHOOPIE PIES

10 tbsp. (5 oz.) unsalted butter, softened

Scant 1 cup (6 oz.) light brown sugar

1 large egg

Scant 3½ cups (12 oz.) all-purpose flour

¼ cup (2 oz.) cocoa powder

½ tsp. baking soda

10 fl. oz. buttermilk

About 2 tsp. red food coloring

MARSHMALLOW FILLING

5 oz. pink marshmallows, snipped into small pieces with scissors

2 tbsp. milk

2 egg whites

2 tbsp. (1 oz.) granulated sugar

MAKES 14

TIP The amount of red coloring you need to add will depend on how brightly tinted you want the finished whoopies to be and how strong your store-bought food coloring is. Paste and powder colors are stronger than liquid colors, with Chinese red food coloring (available from oriental food stores) being the strongest of all.

Elderflowers have the sweet fragrance of plump Muscat grapes. If elderflower cordial is not available, use fresh orange juice instead. The taste will be different but equally delicious.

Strawberry and Elderflower Whoopie Pies

WHOOPIE PIES

10 tbsp. (5 oz.) unsalted butter, softened
¾ cup (5 oz.) granulated sugar
Finely grated zest of 1 small lemon
1 large egg
4 oz. strawberries, hulled and roughly
  chopped
Scant 3 cups (11 oz.) self-rising flour
10½ tbsp. (2 oz.) ground almonds
8 fl oz. sour cream
2 tbsp. elderflower cordial

ELDERFLOWER CREAM FILLING

5 oz. mascarpone
½ pint (4 fl. oz.) heavy cream
2 tbsp. elderflower cordial
Extra strawberries, sliced

MAKES 15

1. Preheat the oven to 350°F. Grease the whoopie pie pans or line two or three baking sheets with baking parchment.

2. To make the whoopie pies, beat the butter and sugar together with the lemon zest until light and creamy. Beat in the egg until evenly combined.

3. Dust the strawberries with a little of the flour. Sift in the rest of the flour, add the ground almonds, and fold in with the sour cream, elderflower cordial and strawberries.

4. Place tablespoons of the mixture in the pans or spaced out on the baking sheets to make 30 pies and bake for 10–12 minutes or until springy to the touch. Cool for 10 minutes, before transferring to a wire rack to cool completely.

5. To make the filling, whisk together the mascarpone, heavy cream, and elderflower cordial until combined and the mixture holds its shape. Use to sandwich the whoopie pies together in pairs with the slices of strawberry.

The smooth blend of coffee both in the cake mix and in the creamy filling makes these whoopies a grown-up treat.

Coffee and Walnut Whoopie Pies with Espresso Cream

1. Preheat the oven to 350°F. Grease the whoopie pie pans or line two or three baking sheets with baking parchment.

2. To make the whoopie pies, put the butter, sugar, egg, vanilla extract, flour, baking soda, sour cream, and milk into a mixing bowl and whisk until smooth and creamy. Stir in the walnuts and coffee.

3. Place tablespoons of the mixture in the pans or spaced out on the baking sheets to make 24 pies and bake for 10 minutes or until springy to the touch. Let cool for 10 minutes before carefully transferring to a wire rack to cool completely.

4. To make the filling, whip the cream until it just holds its shape, then stir in the coffee. Sandwich the whoopie pies together in pairs with the filling. Dust with a little sifted confectioners' sugar before serving.

WHOOPIE PIES
8 tbsp. (4 oz.) unsalted butter, softened
Scant 1 cup (6 oz.) granulated sugar
1 large egg
1 tsp. vanilla extract
Scant 3½ cups (12 oz.) all-purpose flour
1½ tsp. baking soda
10 fl. oz sour cream
4 tbsp. milk
2 oz. chopped walnuts
2 tsp. instant coffee granules mixed with
   1 tbsp. hot water

ESPRESSO CREAM FILLING
2/3 cup (5 fl. oz.) heavy cream
2 tsp. instant coffee granules mixed with
   1 tbsp. hot water

TO DECORATE
Confectioners' sugar, to dust

MAKES 12

Grated orange zest adds a tang to the cream filling, whilst dried apricots and chocolate chips give the whoopie "crusts" extra texture and flavor. If preferred, milk chocolate chips could be used instead of dark.

Apricot and Dark Chocolate Whoopie Pies

1. Preheat the oven to 350°F. Grease the whoopie pie pans or line two or three baking sheets with baking parchment.

2. To make the whoopie pies, cream the butter and sugar together in a mixing bowl until light and fluffy. Add the egg, flour, and milk and stir until smooth and just combined. Stir in the chopped apricots and chocolate chips.

3. Place tablespoons of the mixture in the pans or spaced out on the baking sheets to make 24 pies and bake for 10–12 minutes or until firm to the touch. Let cool for 10 minutes before transferring to a wire rack to cool completely.

4. To make the filling, whip the cream with the orange zest until it holds its shape.

5. Sandwich the whoopie pies together in pairs with the filling.

WHOOPIE PIES

8 tbsp. (4 oz.) unsalted butter, softened
Generous ½ cup (4 oz.) granulated sugar
1 large egg
1 2/3 cups (7 oz.) self-rising flour
2 tbsp. milk
2/3 cup (3½ oz.) ready-to-eat dried
    apricots, snipped into small pieces
2½ tbsp. dark chocolate chips

ORANGE CREAM FILLING

1¼ cup (9 fl. oz.) heavy cream
Finely grated zest of 1 small orange

MAKES 12

The dough for these sophisticated whoopie pies is based on a British macaroon mix with the substitution of hazelnuts rather than the more traditional almonds. Instead of coffee, the buttercream filling could be flavored with cocoa powder or a few drops of almond extract or Amaretto liqueur.

Hazelnut and Coffee Whoopie Pies

1. Preheat the oven to 325°F. Line two baking sheets with baking parchment.

2. To make the whoopie pies, lightly fork the egg whites in a mixing bowl to loosen them, dip the whole hazelnuts in the whites until coated, drain, and set them aside on a small plate.

3. Whisk the egg whites in the bowl until standing in soft peaks. Scatter over the ground hazelnuts, sugar, and semolina and gently fold into the whites using a large metal spoon.

4. Space out teaspoons of the mixture on the baking sheet to make 10 pies, and spread with the back of the spoon. Top half of the teaspoons with a whole hazelnut.

5. Bake for 20 minutes or until pale golden brown. Let cool on the baking sheets for 5 minutes before transferring to a wire rack to cool completely.

6. To make the filling, beat the butter until creamy. Gradually sift in the confectioners' sugar, beating well after each addition and adding the coffee milk to make a smooth icing. Pipe or spread the filling over the plain whoopies and top with those decorated with the hazelnuts. Dust with a little sifted confectioners' sugar.

WHOOPIE PIES

2 large egg whites

10 whole hazelnuts

1 1/3 cup (4 oz.) ground hazelnuts

Scant 1 cup (6 oz.) granulated sugar

2 tbsp. semolina

COFFEE BUTTERCREAM FILLING

8 tbsp. (4 oz.) unsalted butter, softened

1¾ cups (8 oz.) confectioners' sugar

2 tsp. instant coffee granules dissolved in
* 2 tbsp. warm milk*

TO DECORATE

Confectioners' sugar, to dust

MAKES 10

TIP It's important to bake the whoopie dough on baking sheets lined with baking parchment. If spooned into a whoopie pie pan—even one that has been well greased —the whoopie halves will stick and be impossible to remove.

When fresh peaches are in season they can be used instead of canned; but peel off the furry skins before adding the chopped fruit to the mix. To do this, put the peaches in a bowl, cover them with boiling water and leave for about a minute before draining, cooling, and stripping off the skins.

Peach and Coconut Whoopie Pies

WHOOPIE PIES

3 oz. finely chopped fresh or canned
   peach flesh
Scant 3½ cups (12 oz.) all-purpose flour
6 tbsp. (3 oz.) unsalted butter, softened
Scant 1 cup (6 oz.) granulated sugar
1 large egg
1 tsp. baking soda
2 oz. shredded unsweetened coconut
½ pint (8 fl. oz) sour cream
2 tbsp. coconut milk

PEACH AND COCONUT FILLING
   AND TOPPING

9 tbsp. (4½ oz.) unsalted butter, softened
2 cups (9 oz.) confectioners' sugar
3 tbsp. coconut milk
1–2 fresh peaches, stoned, or 4–5 canned
   peach halves, cut into small slices
2 tbsp. shredded unsweetened coconut,
   lightly toasted

MAKES 15

1. Preheat the oven to 350°F. Grease the whoopie pie pans or line two to three baking sheets with baking parchment.

2. To make the whoopie pies, dust the chopped peaches in a little of the flour. Beat the butter and sugar together until creamy. Beat in the egg and then sift in the remaining flour and baking soda. Stir in with the shredded coconut, sour cream, and coconut milk until evenly combined. Finally, fold in the peaches.

3. Place tablespoons of the mixture into the pans or spaced out on the baking sheets to make 30 pies and bake for 10–12 minutes or until just firm. Let cool for 10 minutes, before transferring to a wire rack to cool completely.

4. To make the filling, beat the butter in a mixing bowl until creamy. Gradually sift in the confectioners' sugar, beating well after each addition and adding the coconut milk to make a soft frosting. Use about three-quarters of the frosting to sandwich the whoopie pies in pairs, adding a few peach slices to each filling.

5. Pipe or spread the remaining filling on top of the whoopies, top each with a peach slice and sprinkle over the toasted coconut.

Instead of buttercream you could fill the whoopies with lemon-flavored heavy cream. Simply whip the cream with some finely grated lemon zest until the cream holds its shape.

Lemon Yogurt Whoopie Pies

1. Preheat the oven to 350°F. Grease the whoopie pie pans or line two or three baking sheets with baking parchment.

2. To make the whoopie pies, beat the butter, sugar, and lemon zest together until light and creamy. Beat in the egg until mixed in. Sift the flour and baking soda together. Beat the yogurt and milk together until smooth.

3. Stir the flour into the mixture alternately with the yogurt and milk until evenly combined. Place tablespoons of the mixture in the pans or spaced out on the baking sheets to make 30 pies and bake for 10–12 minutes or until just firm to the touch. Let cool for 10 minutes before transferring to a wire rack to cool completely.

4. To make the filling, beat the butter until creamy. Gradually sift in the confectioners' sugar, beating well after each addition and adding enough lemon juice to give a soft, spreadable icing. Use to sandwich the whoopie pies together in pairs. Serve dusted with confectioners' sugar, if desired.

WHOOPIE PIES

10 tbsp. (5 oz.) unsalted butter, softened
Scant 1 cup (6 oz.) granulated sugar
Finely grated zest of 1 lemon
1 large egg
Scant 3¾ cups (13 oz.) all-purpose flour
½ tsp. baking soda
5 fl. oz. plain Greek yogurt
5 fl. oz. milk

LEMON BUTTERCREAM FILLING

12 tbsp. (6 oz.) unsalted butter, softened
3 cups (12 oz.) confectioners' sugar
2–3 tbsp. lemon juice

TO DECORATE

Confectioners' sugar, to dust (optional)

MAKES 15

The soft dark brown sugar and molasses give these pies a moist texture that complements the lemon zest tang and ginger-spiced flavors wonderfully.

Ginger and Lemon Whoopie Pies

1. Preheat the oven to 350°F. Grease the whoopie pie pans or line two or three baking sheets with baking parchment.

2. To make the whoopie pies, cream together the butter, dark brown sugar, and lemon zest until light and fluffy. Beat in the molasses and egg, then sift in the flour, baking soda, ginger, and cinnamon, stirring until evenly mixed. Finally, stir in the milk.

3. Shape the mixture into 24 small balls, and place them spaced out on the baking sheets, pressing down on them gently to flatten slightly.

4. Bake for 10–12 minutes or until just firm to the touch. Let cool on the baking sheets for 5 minutes before transferring to a wire rack to cool completely.

5. To make the buttercream filling, beat the butter until creamy. Gradually sift in the confectioners' sugar, beating well after each addition, and adding the lemon juice when the mixture looks dry to make a smooth, spreadable icing.

6. Sandwich the whoopie pies together in pairs with the lemon buttercream filling.

WHOOPIE PIES

8 tbsp. (4 oz.) unsalted butter, softened
Scant 1 cup (6 oz.) dark brown sugar
Finely grated zest of 1 lemon
2 tbsp. molasses
1 large egg
Scant 3 cups (11 oz.) all-purpose flour
½ tsp. baking soda
1 tsp. ground ginger
1 tsp. ground cinnamon
9 tbsp. (4½ fl. oz.) milk

LEMON BUTTERCREAM FILLING

8 tbsp. (4 oz.) unsalted butter, softened
1¾ cups (8 oz.) confectioners' sugar
Juice of 1 lemon

MAKES 12

Rosewater is the liquid produced when rose petals are steeped in water which is then distilled. Originating from the Middle East, where it is widely used in cooking (in particular for Turkish Delight); it adds an attractive fragrance to cake mixes.

Vanilla and Rosewater Whoopie Pies

1. Preheat the oven to 350°F. Grease the whoopie pie pans or line two or three baking sheets with baking parchment.

2. To make the whoopie pies, sift the flour and baking soda together. In a mixing bowl, beat the butter and sugar together until creamy. Beat in the vanilla and egg until combined, then stir in the flour a little at a time with the buttermilk.

3. Place tablespoons of the mixture into the pans or spaced out on the baking sheets to make 24 pies and bake for about 15 minutes or until light golden and just firm to the touch. Let cool for 10 minutes before transferring to a wire rack to cool completely.

4. To make the filling, beat the butter until creamy. Gradually sift in the confectioners' sugar, beating well after each addition and adding the vanilla and milk to make a soft icing. Sandwich the whoopies in pairs with the buttercream.

5. To make the glaze, sift the sugar into a bowl and stir in enough lemon juice to make a smooth, spreadable icing. Stir in the rosewater and a few drops of pink food coloring or grenadine syrup to tint the icing a pale pink. Pipe or drizzle the icing over the whoopie pies.

WHOOPIE PIES

Scant 4 cups (14 oz.) all-purpose flour
½ tsp. baking soda
10 tbsp. (5 oz.) unsalted butter, softened
¾ cup (5 oz.) granulated sugar
1 tsp. vanilla extract
1 large egg
10 fl. oz. buttermilk

VANILLA BUTTERCREAM FILLING

12 tbsp. (6 oz.) unsalted butter, softened
3 cups (12 oz.) confectioners' sugar
1 tsp. vanilla extract
3 tbsp. milk

ROSEWATER GLAZE

1¾ cups (8 oz.) confectioners' sugar
About 2 tbsp. lemon juice
1 tsp. rosewater
Few drops of pink food coloring or
  grenadine syrup

MAKES 12

As a special touch, these could be iced pink or blue according to the gender of the new arrival; but if you prefer to break with tradition, tint the icing yellow, orange, green, or any bright color you choose. Decorate the tops with small edible decorations such as animal candy faces.

Baby Shower Whoopie Pies

1. Preheat the oven to 350°F. Grease the whoopie pie pans or line two or three baking sheets with baking parchment.

2. To make the whoopie pies, beat the butter, sugar, and orange zest together in a mixing bowl until light and fluffy. Beat in the egg until combined. Sift in the flour and rice flour and fold in. Finally, mix in the orange juice.

3. Place tablespoons of the mixture in the pans or spaced out on the baking sheets to make 28 pies and bake for 10–12 minutes or until golden brown and springy to the touch. Let cool for 10 minutes before transferring to a wire rack to cool completely.

4. To make the buttercream, beat the butter until creamy. Gradually sift in the confectioners' sugar, beating well after each addition, and stir in enough orange juice to make a soft, spreadable cream. Sandwich the whoopie pies together in pairs with the filling.

5. To make the frosting, sift the sugar into a bowl and stir in about 2 tablespoons cold water to make a smooth icing. Tint the frosting with a few drops of food coloring, as desired. Drizzle or spread the frosting over the whoopies and decorate with sugar sprinkles and small edible decorations.

WHOOPIE PIES

10 tbsp. (5 oz.) unsalted butter, softened
¾ cup (5 oz.) light brown sugar
Finely grated zest of 1 orange
1 large egg
Scant 2½ cups (10 oz.) self-rising flour
6 tbsp. (2 oz.) rice flour
1/3 cup (5½ fl. oz.) orange juice

ORANGE BUTTERCREAM FILLING

8 tbsp. (4 oz.) unsalted butter, softened
1¾ cups (8 oz.) confectioners' sugar
About 2 tbsp. orange juice

TO DECORATE

1¾ cups (8 oz.) confectioners' sugar
Bright food coloring
Sugar sprinkles
Small edible cake decorations

MAKES 14

TIP Novelty cake decorations for weddings, anniversaries, sporting events, or newborn celebrations can be found in stores selling cake-decorating equipment, large supermarkets, or from specialty websites.

WHOOPIE PIES

4 tbsp. (2 oz.) unsalted butter, softened
1/3 cup (3 oz.) granulated sugar
1 large egg
2/3 cup (3 oz.) self-rising flour, sifted
Finely grated zest of 1 small orange

TOPPING

2 tbsp. orange juice
1/4 cup (2 oz.) granulated sugar
Orange crystal sugar

WHITE CHOCOLATE FILLING

5 oz. white chocolate, chopped
6 tbsp. (3 oz.) unsalted butter, softened
1 1/4 cup (5 oz.) confectioners' sugar, sifted
1 tbsp. orange juice

TO DECORATE

Confectioners' sugar, to dust

MAKES 6

You're sure to discover that few will be able to resist the tempting combination of orange and white chocolate in this whoopie recipe.

Orange and White Chocolate Whoopie Pies

1. Preheat the oven to 350°F. Grease the whoopie pie pans or line two or three baking sheets with baking parchment.

2. To make the whoopie pies, beat together the butter, granulated sugar, egg, flour, and orange zest until smooth.

3. Place tablespoons of the mixture in the pans or spaced out on the baking sheets to make 12 pies and bake for 8–10 minutes or until just firm to the touch.

4. While the whoopies are baking, make the topping. Mix the orange juice and granulated sugar together. As soon as the whoopies come out of the oven, spoon the orange juice and sugar over half of them, scatter over a little orange crystal sugar, and let cool for 15 minutes before transferring to a wire rack to cool completely.

5. To make the filling, melt the chocolate in a bowl over a pan of simmering water, stirring until smooth. In another bowl, beat the butter until creamy and gradually beat in the confectioners' sugar. Stir in the melted, cooled chocolate with the orange juice to make a smooth icing. If necessary, chill in the refrigerator until firm enough to spread, stirring occasionally.

6. Spread the plain whoopie halves with the filling and top with the sugar-crusted halves. Sift over a dusting of confectioners' sugar before serving.

Sharp with the tang of lemon and sweet with their drizzle of white icing, these whoopies are destined to be a hit with everyone.

Vanilla and Lemon Curd Whoopie Pies

1. Preheat the oven to 350°F. Grease the whoopie pie pans or line two or three baking sheets with baking parchment.

2. To make the whoopie pies, put the egg and sugar in a mixing bowl and whisk together until thick, pale and creamy. Drizzle the melted butter around the edge of the bowl and fold in with the vanilla using a large metal spoon.

3. Sift in half the flour with the baking soda and fold in with half the buttermilk. Sift in the remaining flour, add the rest of the buttermilk, and fold in until all the ingredients are evenly combined.

4. Place 24 dessert spoons of the mixture in the pans or spaced out on the baking sheets and bake for 12–15 minutes or until springy to the touch. Let cool for 10 minutes before carefully removing from the pan or baking sheet to a wire rack to cool completely.

5. Sandwich the whoopie pies together in pairs with the lemon curd.

6. To make the topping, sift the confectioners' sugar into a bowl and stir in enough lemon juice to give a smooth, spreadable icing. Pipe, drizzle, or spread a little over the top of each whoopie pie and scatter over yellow sugar sprinkles.

WHOOPIE PIES
1 large egg
¾ cup (5 oz.) granulated sugar
6 tbsp. (3 oz.) unsalted butter, melted and cooled
1 tsp. vanilla extract
Scant 2½ cups (10 oz.) all-purpose flour
¾ tsp. baking soda
7 fl. oz. buttermilk

FILLING
8 tbsp. lemon curd

TOPPING
1½ cups (6 oz.) confectioners' sugar
About 2 tbsp. lemon juice
Yellow sugar sprinkles

MAKES 12

These delectable mini-mouthfuls, filled with a rich coffee-flavored mascarpone cream, are ideal for handing round after dinner. But why keep them just for guests when you could indulge yourself by nibbling one—or two—whenever you please?

Mini Chocca-Mocha Whoopies with Mascarpone Cream

WHOOPIE PIES

8 tbsp. (4 oz.) unsalted butter, softened
Scant 1 cup (6 oz.) dark brown sugar
1 large egg
Scant 2½ cups (10 oz.) all-purpose flour
½ tsp. baking soda
¼ cup (2 oz.) cocoa powder, dissolved in
  1 tbsp. hot water and cooled
10 fl. oz. sour cream

MASCARPONE CREAM

3 oz. mascarpone
1¾ cups (8 oz.) sifted confectioners' sugar
4 tbsp. (2 oz.) unsalted butter, softened
1 tsp. instant coffee granules, dissolved in
  2 tbsp. hot water and cooled

MAKES 30

1. Preheat the oven to 350°F. Lightly grease mini-whoopie pie pans (you could bake in batches). Alternatively, line two or three baking sheets with baking parchment.

2. To make the whoopie pies, cream the butter and sugar together in a mixing bowl until light and fluffy. Beat in the egg until mixed in.

3. Sift in the flour and baking soda and stir in with the dissolved cocoa powder and sour cream until combined.

4. Place teaspoons of the mixture in the pans or spaced out on the baking sheets to make 60 pies and bake for 10–12 minutes or until well risen and firm to the touch. Let cool for 10 minutes before transferring to a wire rack to cool completely.

5. To make the mascarpone cream, whisk together the mascarpone, confectioners' sugar, butter, and coffee until smooth. Sandwich the whoopie pies together in pairs with the filling.

A classic British favorite, named after Queen Victoria and shrunk to whoopie pie-size. The mixture will spread too much if spooned onto baking sheets, so bake it in muffin pans. A pan with straight sides to replicate the traditional Victoria sandwich shape is preferable.

Victoria Sandwich Whoopies

WHOOPIE PIES

12 tbsp. (6 oz.) unsalted butter, softened
Scant 1 cup (6 oz.) granulated sugar
3 large eggs
Scant 1½ cups (6 oz.) self-rising flour
1½ tsp. baking powder

CREAM AND JAM FILLING

6 tbsp. strawberry or raspberry jam
Scant 1 cup (7 fl. oz.) whipped heavy cream

TO DECORATE

Granulated sugar, to dust

MAKES 8

1. Preheat the oven to 350°F. Grease a bun pan or a 12-cup cupcake pan.

2. To make the whoopie pies, put the butter, sugar, eggs, flour, and baking powder in a mixing bowl and beat until smooth and creamy.

3. Spoon the mixture into the pans and bake for 10–12 minutes or until golden and springy to the touch. Cool in the trays for 10 minutes before lifting out and transferring to a wire rack to cool completely.

4. To fill the whoopies, beat the jam to loosen it and make it easier to spread over half of the sponges. Top with the whipped cream and the remaining sponges. Dust with granulated sugar before serving.

It's well known that cranberries— whether fresh, dried, or pressed to make a juice—are a healthy addition to any diet. Adding dried berries to these whoopies adds texture and their unique fruity flavor.

Cranberry and Apricot Whoopie Pies

1. Preheat the oven to 350°F. Grease the whoopie pie pans or line two or three baking sheets with baking parchment.

2. To make the whoopie pies, chop the apricot halves into small pieces and dust with a little of the flour. Beat the butter and sugar together in a mixing bowl until light and fluffy. Beat in the egg until mixed in.

3. Sift in the remaining flour and stir in with the dried cranberries and chopped apricot. Place tablespoons of the mixture in the pans or spaced out on the baking sheets to make 30 pies.

4. Bake for 10–12 minutes or until golden brown and just firm to the touch. Let cool for 10 minutes before transferring to a wire rack to cool completely.

5. To make the filling, put the chocolate in a bowl and melt by standing the bowl over a pan of simmering water, stirring until smooth. Beat the butter until creamy and gradually sift in the confectioners' sugar, beating well after each addition. When all the sugar has been added, beat in the melted chocolate and milk. Chill, if necessary, until thick enough to spread.

6. Sandwich the whoopie halves together in pairs. Add a little apricot glaze to the top of each one and sprinkle over the chopped pistachios.

WHOOPIE PIES
5 canned apricot halves, well drained
Scant 3 cups (11 oz.) self-rising flour
12 tbsp. (6 oz.) unsalted butter, softened
¾ cup (5 oz.) light brown sugar
1 large egg
Scant ¾ cup (5 fl. oz.) milk
3 oz. dried cranberries

WHITE CHOCOLATE FILLING AND TOPPING
5 oz. white chocolate, chopped
8 tbsp. (4 oz.) unsalted butter, softened
1¾ cups (8 oz.) confectioners' sugar
2 tbsp. milk
4 tbsp. apricot glaze, warmed
2 tbsp. finely chopped pistachios

MAKES 15

WHOOPIE PIES

1 dessert apple such as Granny Smith,
   peeled, cored, and grated or finely
   chopped
1 tbsp. lemon juice
8 tbsp. (4 oz.) unsalted butter, softened
Scant 1 cup (6 oz.) granulated sugar
1 large egg
Scant 2½ cups (10 oz.) self-rising flour
1 tsp. baking powder
1 tsp. ground cinnamon
10½ tbsp. (2 oz.) ground almonds
¾ cup (6 fl. oz.) milk
3 tbsp. sliced almonds

FILLING

8 tbsp. (4 oz.) unsalted butter, softened
1¾ cups (8 oz.) confectioners' sugar
2 tbsp. lemon juice

MAKES 12

The finely chopped or grated apple creates a deliciously moist texture when combined with soft ground almonds.

Spiced Apple and Almond Whoopie Pies

1. Preheat the oven to 350°F. Grease the whoopie pie pans or line two or three baking sheets with baking parchment.

2. To make the whoopie pies, mix the grated or finely chopped apple with the lemon juice. Put the butter, granulated sugar, and egg in a mixing bowl. Sift in the flour, baking powder, and cinnamon, add the ground almonds and milk and beat for 1–2 minutes with an electric hand whisk or wooden spoon until the mixture is smooth and creamy. Stir in the apple and lemon juice.

3. Place tablespoons of the mixture in the pans or spaced out on the baking sheets to make 24 pies and sprinkle the sliced almonds over half of the shapes. Bake in the oven for 10–12 minutes or until springy to the touch. Let cool for 5 minutes before transferring to a wire rack to cool completely.

4. To make the filling, beat the butter until creamy. Gradually sift in the confectioners' sugar, beating well after each addition until combined, adding the lemon juice to make a soft, spreadable icing.

5. Spread the filling over the plain whoopies and top with the almond-sprinkled pies.

Brown sugar and maple syrup give these whoopies a warm caramel flavor. Pecans add a pleasing crunch to the texture.

Pecan and Maple Whoopie Pies

1. Preheat the oven to 350°F. Grease the whoopie pie pans or line two or three baking sheets with baking parchment.

2. To make the whoopie pies, cream the butter, sugar, and orange zest together in a mixing bowl until light and fluffy. Beat in the egg until mixed in. Sift in the flour and stir in with the maple syrup, milk, and chopped pecans.

3. Place tablespoons of the mixture in the pans or spaced out on the baking sheets to make 24 pies and top half with the pecan halves. Bake for 10–12 minutes or until springy to the touch. Let cool for 10 minutes before carefully removing from the pan or baking sheet to a wire rack to cool completely.

4. To make the filling, beat the butter in a bowl until creamy. Gradually sift in the confectioners' sugar, beating well after each addition. Stir in the maple syrup and milk. Spread the filling over the flat side of the plain whoopies and place those with pecan halves on top.

WHOOPIE PIES

12 tbsp. (6 oz.) unsalted butter, softened
¾ cup (5 oz.) light brown sugar
Finely grated zest of 1 small orange
1 large egg
Scant 3 cups (11 oz.) self-rising flour
5 tbsp. maple syrup
9 tbsp. (4½ fl. oz.) milk
50g (2 oz.) chopped pecans
12 pecan halves

MAPLE BUTTERCREAM FILLING

8 tbsp. (4 oz.) unsalted butter, softened
1 2/3 cup (7 oz.) confectioners' sugar
2 tbsp. maple syrup
1 tbsp. milk

MAKES 12

Who could resist a triple-layered brownie sandwiched with cream cheese frosting? This mixture will spread too much for baking sheets; use whoopie pie pans or bun pans with flat bases and sides.

Triple Brownie and Cream Cheese Whoopies

BROWNIE WHOOPIES

9 oz. dark chocolate, chopped
16 tbsp. (9 oz.) unsalted butter, softened
Scant 1½ cups (9 oz.) dark brown sugar
2 large eggs
Scant 1¼ cups (5 oz.) all-purpose flour
1 tsp. vanilla extract
3¾ tbsp. (2 oz.) finely chopped pecans

CREAM CHEESE FILLING

4 oz. full-fat cream cheese
4 tbsp. (2 oz.) unsalted butter, softened
1¾ cups (8 oz.) confectioners' sugar

TO DECORATE

Cocoa powder, to dust

MAKES 10

1. Preheat the oven to 350°F. Lightly grease three whoopie pie or bun pans (bake the mixture in batches, if necessary).

2. To make the whoopie pies, melt the chocolate in a bowl over a pan of simmering water, stirring until smooth. Beat the butter and sugar together until creamy, then beat in the eggs one at a time, adding a little of the flour if necessary to prevent the mixture from curdling. Add the vanilla and stir in with the melted, cooled chocolate.

3. Sift in the rest of the flour and stir in until just combined. Finally, fold in the pecans.

4. Spoon the mixture into the whoopie pie or bun pans and bake for 15–20 minutes or until a thin crust forms on top but the brownies still feel quite soft to the touch.

5. Let cool in the pans before carefully lifting out. To make the filling, whisk together the cream cheese, butter, and confectioners' sugar until creamy and smooth.

6. Sandwich the brownie stacks of three with the cream cheese frosting. Dust with cocoa powder before serving.

These are too good to keep for Halloween; they could be made out of season using canned, unsweetened pumpkin purée.

Pumpkin and Ginger Whoopie Pies

WHOOPIE PIES

Scant 3½ cups (12 oz.) all-purpose flour
1 tsp. baking soda
1 tsp. ground ginger
1 tsp. pumpkin pie spice
8 tbsp. (4 oz.) unsalted butter, softened
Scant 1 cup (6 oz.) light brown sugar
1 large egg
Generous 1 cup (7 oz.) cooked pumpkin, mashed
2 tbsp. buttermilk or sour cream

GINGER CREAM CHEESE FILLING

9 oz. full-fat cream cheese
3 tbsp. ginger marmalade

MAKES 12

1. Preheat the oven to 350°F. Grease the whoopie pie pans or line two or three baking sheets with baking parchment.

2. To make the whoopie pies, sift together the flour, baking soda, ginger, and pumpkin pie spice. In a mixing bowl, beat the butter and sugar together until creamy. Beat in the egg until combined and then stir in the dry ingredients, mashed pumpkin, and buttermilk or sour cream.

3. Place tablespoons of the mixture in the pans or spaced out on the baking sheets to make 24 pies and bake for 15 minutes or until risen and springy to the touch. Let cool for 10 minutes before transferring to a wire rack to cool completely.

4. To make the filling, mix the cream cheese and the marmalade together. Use to sandwich the whoopie pies in pairs.

Sweet and moist with mashed banana and chopped pineapple, these whoopies are perfect for a flash of excitement and an energy boost to see you through the day.

Banana and Pineapple Whoopie Pies

1. Preheat the oven to 350°F. Grease the whoopie pie pans or line two or three baking sheets with baking parchment.

2. To make the whoopie pies, dust the pineapple with a little of the flour. Sift the remaining flour, the baking powder, and baking soda together. In a mixing bowl, beat the butter and sugar together until creamy and then beat in the egg until combined. Fold in the dry ingredients.

3. Stir the mashed bananas, pineapple, and buttermilk into the mixture. Place tablespoons of the mixture in the pans or spaced out on the baking sheets to make 24 pies and bake for 10–12 minutes or until just firm to the touch. Let cool for 10 minutes before transferring to a wire rack to cool completely.

4. To make the filling, beat the butter until creamy. Sift in the confectioners' sugar a little at a time, beating well after each addition. Finally, beat in the milk and vanilla.

5. Sandwich the whoopie pies together in pairs with the filling.

WHOOPIE PIES

4 oz. fresh or canned pineapple, chopped into small pieces
Scant 2½ cups (10 oz.) all-purpose flour
1 tsp. baking powder
1 tsp. baking soda
8 tbsp. (4 oz.) unsalted butter, softened
Scant 1 cup (6 oz.) light brown sugar
1 large egg
2 small, very ripe bananas, peeled and mashed
3 tbsp. buttermilk

VANILLA BUTTERCREAM FILLING

6 tbsp. (3 oz.) unsalted butter, softened
1¾ cups (8 oz.) confectioners' sugar
1 tbsp. milk
1 tsp. vanilla extract

MAKES 12

Cakepops

Cakepops

If cakepops have as romantic a provenance as whoopie pies, I've yet to discover it. Nonetheless, these miniature treats on a stick—crossing a cake with a lollipop—have become the must-have novelty sweet whenever there is something to celebrate.

Basic cakepop recipes feature dark chocolate cake crumbs with sugar and cream cheese, combining the ingredients until they stick together. The mixture is then shaped into small balls about 1 inch in diameter, pushed on top of lollipop sticks, dipped in a candy coating, decorated with chocolate sprinkles, and left to set.

However, it's more than possible to create lots of variations on the basic mix, and with these recipes I've done just that—using plain sponge or ginger cake crumbs instead of chocolate, substituting butter for cream cheese, and adding dried fruits and nuts.

Sponge Cake for Making Cakepops

You can buy store-bought chocolate cakes (including dry-textured brownies); plain sponge cakes (such as trifle sponges, French madeleines, pound cakes); or ginger cakes (dry-textured, not a sticky gingerbread). Turn these cakes into crumbs by whizzing in a blender. If the cake is left to go slightly dry it will be easier to make into crumbs.

Alternatively, follow the main recipe and simple variations listed opposite to make your own cake base for cakepops.

Candy Coatings

Cakepops are usually dipped in melted candy coating wafers that are available in many different shades and can be bought online, or from cake-decorating stores and larger supermarkets. They tend to be very sweet, so you might prefer to use melted chocolate. Ordinary chocolate takes quite a long time to set so use a good-quality cooking chocolate, which will set more quickly and have a richer taste.

Equipment

If you use a store-bought cake, you will need very little equipment: only a bowl for making your mix, a large plate or baking sheet, lollipop sticks, another bowl for melting the candy coating and—very importantly—a block of Styrofoam to push your cakepop sticks into while the coating sets. If you leave the cakepops to set on a plate the coating will not set evenly.

Plain Sponge Recipe

8 tbsp. (4 oz.) unsalted butter, softened
Generous ½ cup (4 oz.) granulated sugar or soft brown sugar
2 large eggs
Generous 1 cup (4 oz.) self-rising flour
1 tsp. baking powder

1 Preheat the oven to 350°F. Grease and line a 7-inch round or square cake tin with baking parchment.

2 Put all the ingredients in a bowl and whisk or beat together until evenly combined.

3 Spoon the mixture into the tin and bake for about 30 minutes or until a toothpick pushed into the center of the cake comes out clean. Cool for 5 minutes before turning out on to a wire rack to cool completely.

Variations

For a chocolate sponge, add 2 tbsp. cocoa powder dissolved in 2 tbsp. warm milk to the cake mix ingredients.

Making the perfect cakepop

1. Make your cakepop mixture and shape it into small balls. If it is too wet or soft to shape straight away, chill it in the refrigerator for about 30 minutes to 1 hour to firm up. Place the balls on a plate or baking sheet lined with foil or baking parchment and chill for about 1 hour until firm. Don't chill the balls for too long as some mixtures may dry out, crack, and be difficult to dip.

2. Melt your candy coating wafers on defrost setting in the microwave for 3–4 minutes, stirring regularly until smooth. Alternatively, stand the bowl of candy coating wafers over a pan of simmering water without letting the bottom of the bowl touch the water.

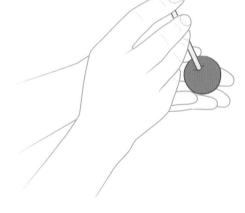

3. Dip the ends of lollipop sticks in the melted candy coating wafers and push into the cake balls. Leave for a minute or so for the sticks to fix in place—this prevents the balls dropping off the sticks when you dip them.

5. Push the sticks into a block of Styrofoam and add sugar sprinkles or other decorations before the coating sets. Don't worry if excess candy coating rolls down any of the sticks before they set, simply wipe the sticks clean with a damp cloth.

6. Cakepops will keep for several days in a cool place. They can be stored in the refrigerator, but they must be covered or the chocolate candy coating will bloom and sweat.

4. Coat the balls in the melted candy coating wafers by holding the stick and dipping them or spooning the coating over them. Twirl or shake the sticks to allow excess coating to drop back into the bowl. If the coating thickens too much before you've dipped all the balls, stir a tablespoon of vegetable oil into it or, if using chocolate, re-melt it.

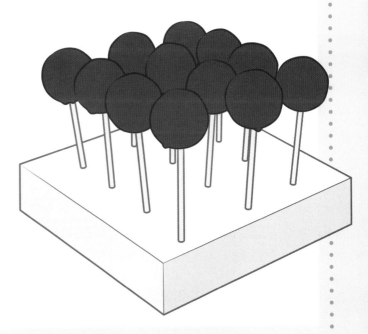

These would be fun to make for a baby shower. If the radiant mom-to-be knows she's expecting a girl, dip the pops in pink melted candy coating wafers and omit the blue food coloring from the cake mix.

Blue Velvet Chocolate Cakepops

CAKEPOPS

5 oz. plain chocolate cake, made into crumbs
1 tbsp. dark brown sugar
3 oz. dark chocolate, melted
6 tbsp. (3 oz.) unsalted butter, melted
1–2 tsp. strong blue food coloring

DIPPING AND DECORATING

12 oz. blue candy coating wafers, melted
Blue sugar sprinkles

MAKES 20

TIP Although made with dark chocolate, the cake mixture should have a noticeably blue tinge to it. Use a strong blue food coloring, preferably a paste coloring, as this will give a bolder shade.

1. To make the cakepops, put the chocolate cake crumbs in a bowl and stir in the sugar, melted dark chocolate, melted butter, and blue food coloring.

2. Put teaspoons of the mixture on a large plate lined with foil or baking parchment and chill until firm enough to roll into small balls. Chill again until they feel firm.

3. Dip the end of a lollipop stick in the melted candy coating wafers and push it into one of the balls. Repeat with the remaining balls and leave for a few minutes until set.

4. Dip the balls in the melted candy coating wafers until evenly coated, letting any excess drip back into the bowl. Push the sticks into a block of Styrofoam, scatter blue sugar sprinkles over each cakepop, and let set.

Forget the flowers and the candy box: cakepops are the modern "must-have" gift for the one you love.

Valentine Cakepops

1. To make the cakepops, beat the cream cheese, butter, and confectioners' sugar together until smooth.

2. Put the cake crumbs in a mixing bowl and gradually work in the cream cheese mixture until combined.

3. Put teaspoons of the mixture onto a large plate lined with baking parchment and chill until firm enough to roll into small balls. Chill again for about 1 hour until firm.

4. Dip the end of a lollipop stick in the melted dark chocolate and push it into the base of one of the balls. Repeat with the remaining balls and leave for a minute or two until the chocolate sets.

5. Dip the balls in the chocolate until evenly coated and push the sticks into a block of Styrofoam. Scatter over the gold sprinkles when almost set. Let set completely before decorating each with a red gum paste heart and white gum paste stars, fixed in place with a little decorating icing.

CAKEPOPS

2 oz. full-fat cream cheese
4 tbsp. (2 oz.) unsalted butter, softened
¾ cup (3½ oz.) confectioners' sugar, plus extra for dusting
11 oz. plain sponge or pound cake, made into crumbs

DIPPING AND DECORATING

1 lb. 2 oz. dark chocolate, melted
Gold sprinkles
Red gum paste hearts
White gum paste or chocolate stars
Decorating icing

MAKES 30

TIP To make the gum paste hearts and stars, roll out red and white gum paste as thinly as possible and cut out small hearts and stars using a sharp knife or heart-shaped and star cutters.

Cakepops can be hidden in all sorts of out-of-sight places for children to find in the Great Easter Egg Hunt. If you don't have time to model the chicks, top the "eggs" with small edible bought decorations.

Easter Egg Cakepops

CAKEPOPS

6 oz. sponge cake, made into crumbs
1 tbsp. granulated sugar
3½ oz. dark chocolate, melted
6 tbsp. (3 oz.) unsalted butter, melted

FILLING, DIPPING, AND DECORATING

1 oz. yellow marzipan
2 oz. white marzipan
1 lb. lavender candy coating wafers,
*   melted*
Soft shimmer pearl sprinkles
Easter chicks (see intro)

MAKES 20

VARIATION You could decorate your eggs with colored gum paste to make pretty center pieces for an Easter table (see previous page).

1. To make the cakepops, put the cake crumbs in a bowl and stir in the sugar, melted dark chocolate, and butter. Knead the mixture until it holds together.

2. To make the filling, divide the yellow marzipan into 20 tiny pieces and shape each one into an egg. Divide the white marzipan into 20 pieces. Mold each white piece around a yellow marzipan piece to make "hard-boiled eggs."

3. Cover with the chocolate crumb mixture, keeping the egg shape. Put on a plate and chill until firm.

4. Dip the end of a lollipop stick in the melted candy coating wafers, then push it into the side of one of the chocolate eggs. Repeat with the remaining eggs and let the candy coating set.

5. Dip the egg pops in the melted candy coating wafers until evenly coated. Push the sticks into a block of Styrofoam, dot with soft shimmer pearl sprinkles, and leave to set. Decorate each one with a small gum paste or marzipan chick, fixed in place with a dab of decorating icing.

Pretty as a picture, these novelty bonnet pops are perfect for an Easter tea tray.

Easter Bonnet Cakepops

1. To make the cakepops, put the sponge cake crumbs in a bowl and stir in the butter, white chocolate, and lemon curd.

2. Shape the mixture into 6 balls, put on a plate lined with foil or baking parchment, and chill until firm enough to cut each ball in half through the center. Return the shapes to the plate and chill again until firm.

3. Dip the end of a lollipop stick in the melted candy coating wafers and push into the base of one of the white chocolate shapes. Repeat with the remaining shapes and leave for a minute or two to set.

4. Dip the white chocolate shapes in the melted candy coating wafers until coated all over, then press the lollipop sticks into a block of Styrofoam. Let set.

5. While the cakepops set, roll out yellow gum paste or petal paste very thinly on a working surface dusted with confectioners' sugar. Cut out 12 rounds about 1 inch larger than the base of the dipped shapes and make a hole in the center of each one with a lollipop stick. Place the rounds on top of small pieces of plastic wrap on a chopping board, tucking the wrap around the diameter of each round so that they dry with a curled brim. Let the rounds dry out and become firm before threading them onto the cakepop sticks. Fix them in place with a dab of decorating icing. Let set.

6. Decorate each cakepop bonnet with small iced flowers, fixed in place with a dab of decorating icing.

CAKEPOPS

6 oz. plain sponge cake, made into crumbs
4 tbsp. (2 oz.) unsalted butter, melted
3 oz. white chocolate, melted
1 tbsp. lemon curd

DIPPING AND DECORATING

12 oz. yellow candy coating wafers, melted
Yellow gum paste or petal paste
Confectioners' sugar, for rolling
Colored decorating icing
Small iced flowers

MAKES 12

Any Mom who loves spring flowers and dark, decadent chocolate is sure to be delighted with a batch of these pretty cakepops on Mother's Day.

Flower Garland Cakepops

CAKEPOPS

5 oz. plain sponge cake, made into crumbs
1 tbsp. dark brown sugar
3 oz. milk chocolate, melted
6 tbsp. (3 oz.) unsalted butter, melted

DIPPING AND DECORATING

12 oz. white chocolate, melted
Small gum paste flowers and leaves

MAKES 16

1. To make the chocolate cakepops, put the sponge cake crumbs in a bowl and stir in the sugar, melted chocolate, and butter.

2. Knead the mixture together and shape it into 16 small balls. Chill the balls on a plate lined with foil or baking parchment until they feel firm.

3. Dip the end of a lollipop stick in the melted white chocolate and push it into one of the balls. Repeat with the remaining balls and leave for a minute or two to set.

4. Dip a ball in the melted white chocolate until evenly coated, then decorate it with a ring of small gum paste flowers, carefully placing the flowers in position with tweezers before the chocolate sets. Repeat with the other cake balls.

5. Push the sticks into a block of Styrofoam and let set.

Once you've mastered making sheep, you can model your cakepops into the heads of any animals you choose—tigers, lions, dogs, pandas... The sky's the limit!

Counting Sheep Cakepops

1. To make the cakepops, put the chocolate and butter in a bowl, stand the bowl over a pan of simmering water and leave until the chocolate and butter have melted. Stir until smooth.

2. In another bowl, beat the cream cheese until smooth. Beat it into the melted chocolate and butter and stir in the sponge cake crumbs until evenly combined. Chill until firm enough to divide into 12 pieces and shape each piece into an oval (these are the sheep's bodies). Chill again until firm.

3. Dip the end of a lollipop stick in the melted candy coating, push into the bottom of one of the ovals, and repeat with the rest. Leave for a few minutes to set and then dip the ovals into the candy coating until evenly coated all over.

4. Push the lollipop sticks into a block of Styrofoam and leave until the chocolate is set. Shape ears from small pieces of black gum paste and fix in place with decorating icing. Shape eyes from white and black gum paste and fix in place with decorating icing. Pipe details on face with white decorating icing and then pipe white curly "wool" over the top of the heads. Leave until the icing is firmly set.

CAKEPOPS

½ cup (4 oz.) dark chocolate chips
4 tbsp. (2 oz.) unsalted butter
2 oz. cream cheese
5 oz. sponge cake, made into crumbs

DIPPING AND DECORATING

11 oz. black candy coating wafers, melted
Black and white gum paste
Black and white decorating icing

MAKES 12

Whether you're celebrating St George's Day, Bastille Day, or the Fourth of July; these red, white, and blue cakepops will liven up any party. If your celebratory occasion of choice isn't suited to any of these colors, simply dip the cakepops in the national colors you need.

Red, White, and Blue Cakepops

CAKEPOPS

6 oz. plain sponge cake, made into crumbs
1 tbsp. granulated sugar
Generous ½ cup (3½ oz.) milk chocolate chips, melted
6 tbsp. (3 oz.) unsalted butter, melted
½ cup (2 oz.) pecans, finely chopped

DIPPING AND DECORATING

6 oz. each of white, red, and blue candy coating wafers
Red and dark blue sugar sprinkles
Small white gum paste stars

MAKES 30

1. To make the cakepops, put the cake crumbs and sugar into a bowl and stir in the melted chocolate, butter, and pecans.

2. Roll the mixture into small balls, put them on a plate lined with foil or parchment paper, and chill in the fridge until firm.

3. Melt the white candy coating wafers. Dip the end of a lollipop stick in the melted candy coating. Push the stick into a ball and repeat with a third of the balls. Leave for a minute or two to set, then dip the balls in the white candy coating until coated. Push the sticks into a block of Styrofoam and sprinkle with red or blue sugar sprinkles. Let set.

4. Repeat with the red and blue candy coating wafers, dipping half the remaining balls in each and decorating the red balls with blue sugar sprinkles and the blue ones with small white gum paste stars. Leave all the pops in the Styrofoam block to set.

Chocolate sprinkles are brilliant for transforming plain cakepops into special treats. You could dip them in any kind of chocolate or try using melted candy coating wafers in your favorite shade.

Polka Dot Cakepops

1. To make the cakepops, put the ginger cake crumbs in a bowl and stir in the brown sugar. Beat together the cream cheese and butter, stir in the orange zest, and gradually mix into the crumbs.

2. Chill the mixture until just firm enough to roll into small balls, put on a plate lined with foil or baking parchment, and chill once more until firm.

3. Dip one end of a lollipop stick in the melted white chocolate and push into one of the balls. Repeat with the remaining balls and leave for a minute or two until set.

4. Dip the balls in the chocolate until evenly coated. Push the sticks into a block of Styrofoam, scattering each cakepop with multicolored chocolate sprinkles before the chocolate sets. Let set.

CAKEPOPS
6 oz. ginger cake, made into crumbs
1 tbsp. light brown sugar
3 oz. full-fat cream cheese
6 tbsp. (3 oz.) unsalted butter, softened
Finely grated zest of 1 small orange

DIPPING AND DECORATION
14 oz. white chocolate, melted
Multicolored chocolate sprinkles

MAKES 20

TIP Use a store-bought ginger cake with a dry texture or one you've made yourself, following the basic sponge cake recipe in the introduction to this chapter and adding 1 teaspoon of ground ginger to the mixture. A sticky Jamaican-style ginger cake would make the mixture too soft.

It won't just be the younger members of the family who fall in love with these friendly bugs, although it's unlikely to stop them biting into them at the first possible moment!

Bumble Bee and Ladybug Cakepops

CAKEPOPS

5 oz. plain sponge cake, made into crumbs
1 tbsp. light brown sugar
3 oz. milk chocolate, melted
3 oz. unsalted butter, melted

TO DECORATE

6 oz. yellow candy coating wafers, melted
6 oz. red candy coating wafers, melted
5 oz. black gum paste
Confectioners' sugar, for rolling out
White, black, and red decorating icing
Small piece of white gum paste

MAKES 16

1. To make the cakepops, put the cake crumbs in a bowl and stir in the sugar, melted chocolate, and melted butter until well mixed.

2. Chill the mixture until firm enough to mold into oval shapes, flattening the bottom of half the shapes to make ladybugs. Put on a plate lined with foil or baking parchment and chill until firm.

3. Put the melted yellow and red candy coating wafers in separate bowls. Dip the end of a lollipop stick in the melted yellow candy coating and press into the center of one of the ovals. Dip another stick in the melted red candy coating and press into one of the flat-based ovals. Repeat with the rest of the shapes.

4. Dip the ovals in the yellow melts to make bumble bees and the flat-based shapes in the red melts to make ladybugs, until evenly coated. Push the sticks into a block of Styrofoam and let set.

5. To decorate the bumble bees, shape heads and stripes from black gum paste and fix in position with decorating icing. Pipe eyes and mouths using white, black, and red decorating icing and shape wings from tiny pieces of white gum paste, fixing them in place with decorating icing.

6. To decorate the ladybugs, roll out small pieces of black gum paste and cut out heads using a small knife. Fix these with decorating icing. Add black spots and pipe on eyes and mouths with white, black, and red decorating icing. Finally, pipe a line of black decorating icing down the back of each ladybug and let set.

One of Australia's favorite cakes gets a cakepop "makeover" in this recipe. Down Under the coconut coating is traditionally left white, but if preferred, give it a light toasting to see it turn a warm gold.

Lamington Cakepops

CAKEPOPS
6 oz. plain sponge cake, made into crumbs
2 tbsp. confectioners' sugar
6 tbsp. (3 oz.) unsalted butter, softened
3 oz. full-fat cream cheese

ICING AND COATING
Scant 2½ cups (14 oz.) milk chocolate, melted
1 cup (3 oz.) flaked, unsweetened coconut

MAKES 20

1. To make the cakepops, mix the cake crumbs and confectioners' sugar together. In a mixing bowl, beat together the butter and cream cheese until smooth and gradually mix into the crumbs until combined.

2. Shape the mixture into 20 balls and place on a large plate lined with foil or baking parchment. Chill until firm.

3. Dip the end of a lollipop stick into the melted milk chocolate and press into the center of one of the balls. Repeat with the rest of the balls and leave for a few minutes to set.

4. Dip all the balls in the melted chocolate and sprinkle over the flaked coconut until evenly coated. Let the chocolate set.

These cakepops will make a great alternative to a traditional birthday cake and will appeal to all ages.

Birthday Cakepops

1. To make the cakepops, put the cake crumbs in a bowl and stir in the sugar, melted chocolate, melted butter and almonds. Roll into small balls, put these on a plate lined with foil or baking parchment and chill until firm.

2. Dip one end of a lollipop stick in the melted milk chocolate and push into one of the balls. Repeat with the remaining balls and leave for a minute or two until set.

3. Dip the balls in the melted chocolate until coated, letting any excess drip back into the bowl. Push the sticks into a block of Styrofoam and scatter multicolored sugar sprinkles over each cakepop. Let set.

4. Fix a small sugar letter to each cakepop with decorating icing. Let set again.

CAKEPOPS

6 oz. plain sponge cake, made into crumbs
1 tbsp. light brown sugar
4 oz. milk chocolate, melted
6 tbsp. (3 oz.) unsalted butter, melted
2 tbsp. finely chopped almonds

DIPPING AND DECORATING

14 oz. milk chocolate, melted
Multicolored chocolate sprinkles
Small alphabet sugar decorations (see Tip)
Decorating icing

MAKES 20

TIP Bags of small sugar letters can be bought from cake-decorating stores or from websites. The letters can be pressed on to the cakepops while the chocolate coating is still wet but, as the cakepops are standing upright, the letters might slide so it's advisable to wait for the chocolate to set, then lay the cakepops down and affix the letters with decorating icing.

Dip the cakepops in melted yellow candy coating wafers. For extra visual pizzazz, you could dip half the batch in yellow and half in green, sprinkling them with contrasting crystal sugar or sprinkles.

Lemon and Lime Cakepops

CAKEPOPS

6 oz. plain sponge cake, made into crumbs
1 tbsp. granulated sugar
Finely grated zest of 1 small lemon and
  1 lime
3 oz. full-fat cream cheese
6 tbsp. (3 oz.) unsalted butter, softened

DIPPING AND DECORATING

14 oz. lime-green candy coating wafers,
  melted
Green and yellow crystal sugar or sugar
  sprinkles

MAKES 20

1. To make the cakepops, put the cake crumbs, sugar, lemon zest, and lime zest in a bowl and stir to mix. In another bowl, beat the cream cheese and butter together, then gradually stir into the crumb mixture.

2. Shape the mixture into 20 balls, put on a large plate lined with foil or baking parchment, and chill in the fridge until firm.

3. Dip the end of a lollipop stick in the melted green candy coating and push into one of the balls. Repeat with the remaining balls and leave for a minute or so to set.

4. Dip the balls in the melted candy coating until coated all over, push the sticks into a block of Styrofoam, and sprinkle the tops of the cakepops with green and yellow crystal sugar or sugar sprinkles. Let set.

Black poppy seeds add a pleasing crunch to baked goods and cakepops are no exception. White poppy seeds are also available but black can make a great contrast with the light cake mix.

Orange and Poppy Seed Cakepops

1. To make the cakepops, put the cake crumbs in a bowl and stir in the orange zest, melted chocolate, melted butter, and poppy seeds. Shape the mixture into small balls, put on a plate lined with foil or baking parchment, and chill until firm.

2. Dip the end of a lollipop stick into the melted candy coating wafers and push it into one of the balls. Repeat with the remaining balls and leave for a minute or two to fix the sticks in place.

3. Dip the balls in the candy coating wafers until evenly coated. Push the sticks into a block of Styrofoam and let set. Pipe a spiral over each cakepop using chocolate decorating icing or melted dark chocolate spooned into a small paper piping bag. Leave to set.

CAKEPOPS
6 oz. plain sponge cake, made into crumbs
Finely grated zest of 1 orange
Generous ½ cup (3½ oz.) white chocolate chips, melted
6 tbsp. (3 oz.) unsalted butter, melted
2 tbsp. poppy seeds

DIPPING AND DECORATING
12 oz. orange candy coating wafers, melted
Chocolate decorating icing or melted dark chocolate

MAKES 16

Pistachios are one of my all-time favorite nuts as not only do they taste sublime, but their subtle green color brightens up all sorts of savory and sweet dishes from pilafs and salads to gateaux, desserts, and, of course, cakepops.

Toffee and Pistachio Cakepops

CAKEPOPS

6 oz. plain sponge cake, made into crumbs
¼ cup (1 oz.) finely chopped pistachios
6 tbsp. (3 oz.) unsalted butter, softened
3 oz. dulce de leche

DIPPING AND DECORATING

14 oz. toffee-flavored buttons or candy coating wafers, melted
Pistachios, chopped
Mini fudge cubes or similar candies

MAKES 20

1. To make the cakepops, mix together the cake crumbs and pistachios. Beat together the butter and dulce de leche and gradually stir into the crumb mixture until it sticks together.

2. Shape the mixture into small balls and chill until firm.

3. Dip the end of a lollipop stick in the melted toffee buttons or candy coating wafers and push it into one of the balls. Repeat with the remaining balls and leave for a few minutes until set.

4. Dip all the balls in the melted mixture, sprinkle over the chopped pistachios and mini fudge cubes. Push into a block of Styrofoam. Let set.

Chocolate lovers will vote these their favorite cakepops as not one, not two, but three different chocolates are all on one stick. Swirl the cakepops as you drizzle over the white chocolate to give a marbled effect.

Triple Chocolate Cakepops

1. To make the cakepops, beat the cream cheese and confectioners' sugar together until smooth.

2. Put the cake crumbs in a mixing bowl and gradually work in the cream cheese and sugar until combined.

3. Shape the mixture into 12 small balls, dusting your hands with confectioners' sugar if it is sticky. Chill in the fridge for 2–3 hours or until firm.

4. Dip the end of a lollipop stick in the melted milk chocolate and press into one of the balls. Repeat with the remaining balls and leave for a few minutes to set.

5. Dip all the balls in the melted milk chocolate until evenly coated and press into a block of Styrofoam.

6. Before the milk chocolate sets, pipe or drizzle over the white chocolate, turning the lollipop sticks to marble the milk and white chocolate together. Let set.

CAKEPOPS

2 oz. full-fat cream cheese

¾ cup (3½ oz.) confectioners' sugar, plus extra for dusting

11 oz. chocolate cake, made into crumbs

DIPPING AND DECORATING

1lb. 2 oz. milk chocolate, melted

3 oz. white chocolate, melted

MAKES 30

Cakepop regulars won't need much convincing that the porridge oats and raisins in these nut-studded delights give them healthy credentials. The oats also give them a pleasingly chewy texture.

Oat and Raisin Cakepops

CAKEPOPS

8 tbsp. (4 oz.) unsalted butter

1 tbsp. brown sugar

2 tbsp. corn syrup

½ cup (3 oz.) dark chocolate chips, melted

2 tbsp. oats

5 oz. sponge cake, made into crumbs

1½ tbsp. raisins

Dipping and decorating

12 oz. milk chocolate, melted

2 tbsp. finely chopped nuts, lightly toasted

MAKES 15

1. To make the cakepops, put the butter, sugar, corn syrup, and chocolate chips in a pan and heat gently until melted. Remove from the heat and stir in the oats, sponge cake crumbs, and raisins, mixing well.

2. Chill the mixture until firm enough to shape into small balls. Place the balls on a plate lined with foil or baking parchment and chill again until they are firm.

3. Dip the end of a lollipop stick in the melted milk chocolate and push it into one of the balls. Repeat with the rest of the balls and leave for a few minutes to set.

4. Dip a ball in the melted chocolate to evenly cover, letting any excess drip back into the bowl. Sprinkle a few chopped nuts over the cakepop and push the stick into a block of Styrofoam. Repeat with the remaining pops. Let set.

If you prefer smooth peanut butter, use that instead of crunchy in the cakepop mix. The pops can also be dipped in colored candy coating wafers—orange would work well—and sprinkled with finely chopped salted peanuts to give a pleasing contrast of sweet–salty flavors.

Peanut and Ginger Cakepops

1. To make the cakepops, put the ginger cake crumbs in a bowl. In another bowl, beat the butter until creamy and then beat in the peanut butter and maple syrup. Stir into the cake crumbs until evenly mixed.

2. Put heaped teaspoons of the mixture on a large plate lined with foil or baking parchment and chill for about 30 minutes or until firm enough to roll into small balls. Place the balls on a plate and chill again for about 1 hour or until firm.

3. Dip the end of a lollipop stick in the melted chocolate and push into one of the balls. Repeat with the remaining balls and leave for a few minutes until set.

4. Dip all the balls in the melted chocolate until evenly coated, letting any excess drip back into the bowl. Push the sticks into a block of Styrofoam, scatter sugar sprinkles over the pops, and let set.

CAKEPOPS
6 oz. ginger cake, made into crumbs
6 tbsp. (3 oz.) unsalted butter, softened
3½ tbsp. (2 oz.) crunchy peanut butter
1 tbsp. maple syrup

DIPPING AND DECORATING
12 oz. milk chocolate, melted
Multicolored sugar sprinkles

MAKES 18

Before chopping very finely and adding to the mix, rinse off the candied cherries sticky syrup coating with warm water and pat dry.

Cherry and Almond Cakepops

CAKEPOPS

6 tbsp. (3 oz.) unsalted butter, softened

3 oz. full-fat cream cheese

5 oz. plain sponge cake, made into crumbs

¼ cup (1 oz.) ground almonds

6 candied cherries, very finely chopped

DIPPING AND DECORATING

1 lb. dark chocolate, melted

Flaked almonds

Red crystal sugar or sugar sprinkles

MAKES 24

1. To make the cakepops, beat the butter and cream cheese together until smooth. Put the cake crumbs and ground almonds in a bowl and gradually mix in the butter and cream cheese. Finally, stir in the chopped candied cherries.

2. Roll the mixture into small balls, place on a plate lined with foil or baking parchment, and chill until firm.

3. Dip the end of a lollipop stick in the melted dark chocolate and push into one of the balls. Repeat with the remaining balls and leave for a few minutes to set.

4. Dip the balls in the melted chocolate until coated, letting the excess drip back into the bowl. Push the sticks into a block of Styrofoam and top each cakepop with a sprinkling of flaked almonds and red crystal sugar or sugar sprinkles. Let set.

"Everything's coming up roses," as the song goes; but when it comes to cakepops, sunflowers are my favorite bloom. Serve these with after-dinner coffee as a bouquet in a tall, narrow-necked vase: a lovely option for petits fours.

Sunflower Cakepops

1. To make the cakepops, put the sponge cake crumbs in a bowl and stir in the sugar, melted dark chocolate, melted butter, and sunflower seeds. Shape the mixture into 20 balls, flatten them at the bottom, and put on a plate lined with foil or baking parchment. Chill in the fridge until firm.

2. Dip the end of a lollipop stick in the melted milk chocolate, push into the base of a ball, and repeat with the rest of the balls. Leave for a minute or so until set.

3. Dip the balls in the chocolate until coated, press the stick into a block of Styrofoam and top each ball with chocolate sprinkles. Leave until the chocolate has set.

4. Roll out yellow gum paste or petal paste thinly on a surface dusted with confectioners' sugar and, using a large flower cutter, cut out 40 flowers. Gather up and re-roll the trimmings as necessary. Make a hole in the center of each flower with a lollipop stick and place the flowers in a bun tray so they dry in a cup shape.

5. When the flowers have dried enough to hold their shape, pipe a little decorating icing around the center holes and push two flowers on to each stick, molding them gently round the bottom of the cakepops. Let set.

CAKEPOPS

6 oz. plain sponge cake, made into crumbs
1 tbsp. granulated sugar
*Generous ½ cup (3½ oz.) dark chocolate
   chips, melted*
6 tbsp. (3 oz.) unsalted butter, melted
1 tbsp. sunflower seeds

DIPPING AND DECORATING

14 oz. milk chocolate, melted
Chocolate sprinkles
12 oz. yellow gum paste or petal paste
Confectioners' sugar, for rolling out
A little decorating icing

MAKES 20

TIP Petal paste is similar to gum paste but dries out much more quickly and sets much harder. You can buy petal paste from cake-decorating stores or online.

Dried fruit works well in cakepop mixes but you do need to chop any large fruit pieces with kitchen scissors or you'll end up with lumpy, irregular-shaped pops. They'll still taste wonderful, though.

Chocolate Blueberry Cakepops

CAKEPOPS

6 tbsp. (3 oz.) unsalted butter, softened

3 oz. full-fat cream cheese

5 oz. plain sponge or pound cake, made into crumbs

¼ cup (1 oz.) ground almonds

2 tbsp. dried blueberries

DIPPING AND DECORATING

14 oz. lavender candy coating wafers, melted

Small blue or lavender and white icing flowers

Lilac shimmer dusting powder

MAKES 20

1. To make the cakepops, beat the butter and cream cheese together until smooth. Put the cake crumbs, ground almonds, and dried blueberries together in a bowl and gradually mix in the creamed mixture.

2. Roll into small balls, put them on a plate lined with foil or baking parchment, and chill in until firm.

3. Dip the end of a lollipop stick in the melted candy coating wafers and push into one of the balls. Repeat with the rest of the balls and leave for a minute or two to set.

4. Dip the balls in the melted candy coating wafers and push the sticks into a block of Styrofoam. Top each cakepop with an icing flower and a dusting of lilac shimmer powder. Let set.

These cakepops are definitely for grown ups. You could try replacing the rum with fruit juice, then all the family could enjoy them.

Spicy Jamaican Rum Cakepops

1. To make the cakepops, mix together the cake crumbs, shredded coconut, sugar, and melted butter. Stir in the rum. Chill the mixture until firm enough to shape into small balls. Put the balls on a plate lined with foil or baking parchment and chill again until firm.

2. Dip the end of a lollipop stick in the melted candy coating wafers or buttons and push into one of the balls. Repeat with the remaining balls and leave for a few minutes until set.

3. Dip all the balls in the melted candy coating wafers or buttons until evenly coated. Push the sticks into a block of Styrofoam and decorate with gold pearl sprinkles or other sugar sprinkles before the coating sets.

CAKEPOPS

5 oz. ginger cake, made into crumbs
2 oz. shredded unsweetened coconut
1 tbsp. light brown sugar
8 tbsp. (4 oz.) unsalted butter, melted
1 tbsp. dark rum

DIPPING AND DECORATING

14 oz. orange candy coating wafers or
orange-flavor buttons, melted
Soft gold pearl sprinkles

MAKES 20

As well as making these frighteningly delicious ghosts for a Halloween party, you could also mold pumpkin-shaped cakepops, dip them in melted orange candy coating wafers then pipe on suitable features with black decorating icing. Displayed in a block of Styrofoam covered with black tissue paper, they'll be an instant hit.

Halloween Ghost Cakepops

CAKEPOPS

5 oz. plain chocolate cake, made into crumbs

1 tbsp. dark brown sugar

3 oz. dark chocolate, melted

6 tbsp. (3 oz.) unsalted butter, melted

2 tbsp. finely chopped dried apricots

DIPPING AND DECORATING

2 1/3 cups (14 oz.) white chocolate chips, melted

Black and red decorating icing

MAKES 18

TIP You could choose to break up chocolate brownies for the cake crumbs. Choose ones that have a dry texture rather than those with a soft, melting center.

1. To make the cakepops, put the cake crumbs in a bowl and stir in the sugar, melted chocolate, butter, and chopped apricots.

2. Put teaspoons of the mixture onto a plate lined with foil or baking parchment and chill until firm enough to shape into balls. Mold the balls into bell shapes, rounding the tops and flattening the bases. Put on a plate and chill once more until firm.

3. Dip the end of a lollipop stick in the melted white chocolate and push into the base of one of the bell shapes. Repeat with the remaining shapes and leave for a minute or two to set.

4. Dip the shapes in the melted white chocolate until evenly coated, letting any excess drip back into the bowl. Push the sticks into a block of Styrofoam and leave until set.

5. Decorate with blobs of black decorating icing for eyes and red decorating icing for mouths. Leave in the Styrofoam block to set.

The perfect gifts for a feline-loving friend. The cats needn't be black as the cakepops can be dipped in white, orange, or brown melted candy coating wafers to make tabbies, calico cats, or ginger toms.

Lucky Black Cat Cakepops

1. To make the cakepops, put the chocolate cake crumbs in a bowl and stir in the sugar, melted milk chocolate, and melted butter.

2. Stir everything together until combined. Place teaspoons of the mixture onto a large plate lined with foil or baking parchment and chill until firm enough to roll into balls. Chill once more until firm.

3. Dip the end of a lollipop stick in the melted candy coating wafers and push it into one of the balls. Repeat with the remaining balls and leave for a few minutes until set.

4. Dip the balls in the melted candy coating wafers until evenly coated, letting any excess drip back into the bowl. Push the sticks into a block of Styrofoam and let set.

5. Shape 40 ears from tiny pieces of black gum paste and fix in place with a dab of black decorating icing. Shape 20 small bows from red gum paste and fix to the base of each cakepop with a little black or red decorating icing. Pipe on eyes with white, green, and black decorating icing, mouths with red icing and whiskers with white icing. Let set.

CAKEPOPS

5 oz. plain chocolate cake, made into crumbs
1 tbsp. dark brown sugar
3 oz. milk chocolate, melted
6 tbsp. (3 oz.) unsalted butter, melted

DIPPING AND DECORATING

14 oz. black candy coating wafers, melted
Black and red gum paste
Black, red, white, and green decorating icing

MAKES 20

These cakepops in the shape of miniature Christmas trees will brighten up any festive celebration. To get you into the seasonal spirit you could add a spoonful of brandy to the cakepop mix.

Christmas Tree Cakepops

1. Put the cake crumbs in a bowl and stir in the sugar, melted chocolate, melted butter, and ground almonds.

2. Chill the mixture until it is firm enough to shape into small cones. Put the cones onto a plate lined with foil and parchment paper and chill for 1 hour or until firm.

3. Dip the end of a lollipop stick in the melted green candy coating wafers and press into the center of the base of one of the cake cones. Repeat with the rest of the cones and leave for a few minutes until set.

4. Dip all the cones in the green candy coating wafers until evenly coated. Roughen up the coating a little to resemble Christmas tree branches. Fix a star on the top of each "tree" and white sugar sprinkles on the "branches" before the candy coating hardens. Push the lollipop sticks into a block of Styrofoam and let set.

CAKEPOPS

5 oz. plain sponge cake, made into crumbs
1 tbsp. dark brown sugar
3 oz. dark chocolate, melted
3 oz. unsalted butter, melted
2 oz. ground almonds

DIPPING AND DECORATING

14 oz. green candy coating wafers, melted
12 small stars cut from thinly rolled yellow gum paste or yellow star-shaped sprinkles
White sugar sprinkles

MAKES 20

TIP If you find it easier, you can affix the stars and silver-colored balls to the trees with a little decorating icing after the melted candy coating wafers have set.

Star-shaped sprinkles made from sugar or chocolate are available from large supermarkets with the baking ingredients. You can also buy them from cake-decorating suppliers or specialists online.

Star Bright Cakepops

CAKEPOPS

6 oz. plain sponge cake, made into crumbs
6 tbsp. (3 oz.) unsalted butter, softened
3½ tbsp. (2 oz.) smooth peanut butter
1 tbsp. honey

DIPPING AND DECORATING

14 oz. white chocolate, melted
Edible silver balls
Star-shaped sugar or chocolate sprinkles

MAKES 20

1. To make the cakepops, put the cake crumbs in a bowl. In another bowl, beat together the butter, peanut butter, and honey until evenly combined and gradually mix into the cake crumbs.

2. Chill the mixture until it is firm enough to roll into small balls, put them on a plate lined with foil or baking parchment and chill until firm.

3. Dip one end of a lollipop stick in the melted chocolate and push into one of the balls. Repeat with the remaining balls and leave for a minute or two until set.

4. Dip the balls in the candy coating wafers until evenly coated. Push the sticks into a block of Styrofoam and sprinkle with a few tiny silver balls. Using tweezers to position them, decorate each cakepop with star-shaped sugar sprinkles. Let set.

...owboarders
...ay as they
glide dow...

Beanie Hat Cakepops

1. To make the cakepops, put the cake crumbs in a bowl and stir in the sugar, melted chocolate, and melted butter. Stir until mixed, then chill the mixture until just firm enough to shape into small cones with slightly flattened points. Put on a plate lined with foil or baking parchment and chill until firm.

2. Dip the end of a lollipop stick in the melted orange candy coating wafers and push into the base of one of the cones. Repeat with the remaining cones and leave for a minute or so to set.

3. Dip the cones in the candy coating wafers until coated and top each one with a malted chocolate sweet. Brush the bottom edge of each cone with melted apricot glaze and roll in the white sugar sprinkles. Push the lollipop sticks into a block of Styrofoam and let set.

CAKEPOPS

6 oz. chocolate cake, made into crumbs
1 tbsp. dark brown sugar
Generous ½ cup (3½ oz.) milk chocolate chips, melted
6 tbsp. (3 oz.) unsalted butter, melted

DIPPING AND DECORATION

14 oz. orange candy coating wafers, melted
12 chocolate malt balls like Maltesers or Whoppers
A little apricot glaze, melted
White sugar sprinkles

MAKES 20

TIP Cool the apricot glaze before brushing it around the bottom of the cones as if it is hot, it will melt the candy coating.

Home-made gifts are always the best, and cakepops shaped like presents are even better.

All Wrapped Up Cakepop Parcels

CAKEPOPS

115 g (4 oz.) dark chocolate, chopped
4 tbsp. (2 oz.) unsalted butter
2 oz. cream cheese
3 tbsp. (1 oz.) walnuts, finely chopped
Scant ¼ cup (1½ oz.) candied cherries, finely chopped
2 oz. golden raisins
4 oz. Graham crackers, crushed into coarse crumbs

DIPPING AND DECORATING

1lb. 4 oz. red candy coating wafers, melted
Colored decorating icing

MAKES 24

1. To make the cakepops, put the chocolate and butter in a bowl, stand the bowl over a pan of simmering water and heat until the chocolate and butter have melted, stirring until completely smooth.

2. In another bowl, beat the cream cheese until smooth and then beat it into the melted chocolate mixture. Stir in the walnuts, cherries, golden raisins, and crushed crackers until evenly combined.

3. Line a small shallow tin or 7 x 4-inch dish with plastic wrap and spoon the mixture into it, spreading it out in an even layer about 1 inch deep and smoothing the top with the back of the spoon. Chill until firm enough to cut into 24 squares.

4. Dip the end of a lollipop stick in the melted candy coating wafers and push into one of the squares. Repeat with the remaining squares and leave for a few minutes to set.

5. Dip the squares in the melted candy coating wafers until evenly coated all over. Push the lollipop sticks into a block of Styrofoam and leave until the coating is firmly set. Pipe ribbons over the cakepops using different colored decorating icing to resemble small parcels.

One bite of these sparkling delights will convince you that you've heard the crunch of feet walking through deep snow outside, even if it's the wrong season and the sun is shining!

Frosted Snowball Cakepops

1. To make the cakepops, put the cake crumbs in a bowl and stir in the sugar, melted chocolate, and melted butter.

2. Drop heaped teaspoonfuls of the mixture onto a plate lined with foil or baking parchment, and chill until firm enough to roll into small balls. Chill again until firm.

3. Dip the end of a lollipop stick in the melted white chocolate or candy coating wafers and push it into one of the balls. Repeat with the remaining balls and leave for a few minutes until the chocolate has set.

4. Dip one ball in the melted white chocolate until evenly coated, then dust with frosted white sugar sprinkles. Use tweezers to place small silver balls on top of the cakepop before the chocolate sets. Repeat with the remaining cakepops.

5. Push the sticks into a block of Styrofoam and let set.

CAKEPOPS

6 oz. plain sponge cake, made into crumbs
1 tbsp. granulated sugar
Generous ½ cup (3½ oz.) white chocolate
  chips, melted
6 tbsp. (3 oz.) unsalted butter, melted

DIPPING AND DECORATING

14 oz. white chocolate or white candy
  coating wafers, melted
Frosted white sugar sprinkles
Small silver balls

MAKES 20

The Italian sweet bread panettone is a buttery Christmas specialty; if you can't track one down at other times of the year, make the cakepops with crumbled brioche or the crumbs of another sweet bake.

Citrus Panettone Cakepops

CAKEPOPS

8 oz. plain panettone, made into crumbs
2 tbsp. granulated sugar
Finely grated zest of 1 small orange
3 oz. full-fat cream cheese
4 tbsp. (2 oz.) unsalted butter, softened

DIPPING AND DECORATING

14 oz. yellow candy coating wafers, melted
Yellow crystal sugar or sprinkles
Orange jelly candies or jelly beans

MAKES 20

TIP Panettone is a sweet Italian bread, originally from Milan, with a light texture that is often studded with golden raisins and candied fruits. When making the crumbs, any dried or candied fruit can be left in the mix.

1. To make the cakepops, mix together the panettone crumbs, granulated sugar, and orange zest.

2. In another bowl, beat together the cream cheese and butter. Gradually mix the creamed mixture into the crumbs until everything sticks together.

3. Roll the mixture into small balls, place on a plate lined with foil or baking parchment, and chill until firm.

4. Dip the end of a lollipop stick in the melted candy coating wafers and push into one of the balls. Repeat with the remaining balls and leave for a few minutes until set.

5. Dip all the balls in the melted candy coating until evenly coated. Push into a block of Styrofoam and decorate with yellow crystal sugar or sprinkles. Top with orange jelly candies or other small candies and let set.

If your friends aren't familiar with popping candy— or "space dust" as it is also known—you can wake up their taste buds with these colorful cakepops. Have some fun seeing their reaction as they find them literally "popping" in their mouths.

Popping Chocolate Cakepops

1. To make the cakepops, put the sponge cake crumbs in a bowl and stir in the sugar, melted chocolate, melted butter, and chopped chocolate honeycomb bar. When evenly mixed, shape into small balls, put on a plate lined with foil or baking parchment, and chill until set.

2. To make the dipping chocolate, put the milk chocolate chips in a bowl and set it over a pan of simmering water. Leave until melted, stirring until smooth.

3. Remove the bowl from the pan and let cool. Dip the end of a lollipop stick in the melted chocolate and push into one of the balls. Repeat with the remaining balls and leave for a minute or two until set.

4. Stir the popping candy into the melted chocolate until all the crystals are coated. Dip the balls in the chocolate to cover them evenly. Let any excess chocolate drip back into the bowl.

5. Push the sticks into a block of Styrofoam and decorate each cakepop with multicolored sugar sprinkles and jelly beans. Let set.

CAKEPOPS

6 oz. plain sponge cake, made into crumbs
1 tbsp. dark brown sugar
Generous ½ cup (3½ oz.) milk chocolate chips, melted
4 tbsp. (2 oz.) unsalted butter, melted
1½ oz. chocolate honeycomb bar, finely chopped

DIPPING AND DECORATING

2 1/3 cups (14 oz.) milk chocolate chips, melted
3 tbsp. popping candy (see Tip)
Multicolored sugar sprinkles
Jelly beans

MAKES 20

TIP Popping candy is sold with other candies at large stores, supermarkets, or from specialized websites. Because contact with water makes the candy lose its ability to "pop," the crystals must be coated completely with melted, cooled chocolate before being added to a cakepop coating or cake mixture.

Index

Acknowledgments

The author would like to thank Kerry Bailey and Jo Lelean for all their help. Special thanks also go to Judith Ferguson.